PRAISE

ANGELS
on
EARTH

"This shining book gives us story after story reminding us that God is always near."

—Roma Downey

"This book proves that there really are angels among us: those unsung heroes who quietly change the lives of others and elevate us all as a result. Few people highlight the beauty of humanity as eloquently and lovingly as Laura does."

—Monica Crowley, PhD, anchor and analyst, Fox News Channel;
editor and columnist, *The Washington Times*

"A powerful testament to the undeniable truth that there is a great force of love guiding our lives and our connections to one another here on earth . . . It will inspire you to embrace the knowing that we can all serve as vehicles of God—and be angels on one another's life journeys here on earth."

—Laura Lynne Jackson, *New York Times* bestselling
author of *The Light Between Us*

"A beautifully written testament to the life-changing power of a simple act of kindness. This book is proof that despite the news headlines, there really is so much good in the world."

—Yvette Manessis Corporon, internationally bestselling
author of *When the Cypress Whispers*

ALSO BY LAURA SCHROFF

An Invisible Thread

An Invisible Thread Christmas Story

ANGELS
on
EARTH

INSPIRING REAL-LIFE STORIES
of Fate, Friendship, and the Power of Kindness

LAURA SCHROFF
and Alex Tresniowski

HOWARD BOOKS
AN IMPRINT OF SIMON & SCHUSTER, INC.

New York   London   Toronto   Sydney   New Delhi

Howard Books
An Imprint of Simon & Schuster, Inc.
1230 Avenue of the Americas
New York, NY 10020

First Howard Books paperback edition October 2017

HOWARD and colophon are trademarks of Simon & Schuster, Inc.

For information about special discounts for bulk purchases, please contact
Simon & Schuster Special Sales at 1-866-506-1949 or
business@simonandschuster.com.

The Simon & Schuster Speakers Bureau can bring authors to your live event.
For more information or to book an event, contact the Simon & Schuster
Speakers Bureau at 1-866-248-3049 or visit our website at
www.simonspeakers.com.

Interior design by Devan Norman

Manufactured in the United States of America

3 5 7 9 10 8 6 4 2

Library of Congress Cataloging-in-Publication Data is available.

ISBN 978-1-5011-4475-2
ISBN 978-1-5011-4523-0 (pbk)
ISBN 978-1-5011-4472-1 (ebook)

To all the angels on earth who are changing lives and making a difference by sharing kindness through human connections.

CONTENTS

CONTENTS

INTRODUCTION

My first act of kindness, or at least the first one I can remember, was putting money in the collection basket during Sunday mass.

I was too young to really understand what the money was for, other than it was somehow helping the less fortunate. I just liked the act of dropping some coins my mother gave me into the basket when it finally reached me. I also remember that not eating or drinking all morning before mass—a requirement back then—usually caused me to pass out in my pew not long after my little act of kindness.

As a young girl I also really liked angels, and I'd wonder if I'd ever be able to glimpse one, hovering over me, feathery wings fluttering in the air. Much later, as an adult, when my mother passed away, I began to think about angels again. In the years after I lost her, I still felt my mother's presence in my life, watching over me, helping me, rooting me on. I could believe my mother had *become* an angel—my protector, my guardian, my guide through both the good times and the hardships of life.

Kindness and angels—I still spend a lot of time thinking about those two things today. In a way they've become the theme of my life, and certainly the theme of the book you are reading right now. Now I'm not any kind of expert in these matters. I've never studied angelology (yes, there is such a thing), nor do I have any special training in the psychology of kindness. The reason I am writing to you about them now is that over the last five years, I have been on a kind of journey that has given me a new understanding of the role of kindness and angels in our lives.

Of what it means to *be* an angel.

You see, I still believe in angels in the traditional sense—celestial beings with beautiful, fluffy wings.

But I've now learned there is another kind of angel, and over the last five years I have seen these angels everywhere.

These are the angels on earth.

And one of them is you.

In 2011 I wrote a book called *An Invisible Thread*. It was about an extraordinary moment that happened in September 1986, when I was thirty-five and a successful ad sales executive living and working in New York City. That day, I passed a homeless eleven-year-old panhandler begging for money on the corner of 56th Street and Broadway.

"Excuse me, lady," he said to me. "Do you have any spare change? I am hungry."

I kept walking. There were lots of homeless people on the streets in New York City in the 1980s, and it was easy just to keep my head down and ignore them. But as I walked away from the boy, something clicked in my head. It was his words, his simple declaration to me.

"I am hungry."

I stopped in the middle of Broadway, turned around, and went back to the boy, whose name was Maurice Mazyck. I offered to buy him lunch at a McDonald's around the corner, and I asked if

I could join him. I soon learned he hadn't eaten anything in two days. That was our first meal together—Big Mac, french fries, and a chocolate shake, extra thick—but not our last. We wound up meeting for dinner the following Monday, and every Monday for the next four years, and hundreds of times after that. We lived only two blocks apart—me in a luxury high-rise, Maurice in a no-torious welfare hotel riddled with drugs and crime—but we might as well have lived on different planets.

Even so, Maurice and I became friends, and that friendship is still going strong today, exactly thirty years later.

The story of how our unlikely friendship grew and changed both of us is the story I told in *An Invisible Thread*. The title is from an ancient Chinese proverb: *An invisible thread connects those who are destined to meet, regardless of time, place, or circumstance. The thread may stretch or tangle, but it will never break.* I chose that title because to me, it perfectly captured the essence of the friendship I share with Maurice. In a busy city of eight million people, on a street corner where literally thousands of people passed Maurice every day without so much as a glance, somehow we found each other at just the moment we most *needed* to find each other.

And everything that was to follow started with the simplest and smallest of gestures—me turning around and going back. Nothing dramatic, certainly nothing heroic. Still, that one, tiny moment changed everything. Some people call such a moment fate. Some call it destiny. Some refer to it as the hand of God at work.

I chose to think of it as an invisible thread—something larger than either Maurice or me steering us into each other's paths, pulling us together.

Our meeting had a profound effect on both our lives, but what I would come to learn is that the real gift of that moment was not from me to Maurice, though I helped him chase a dream he never thought he could have.

It wasn't even from Maurice to me, though his friendship has been one of the great blessings of my life.

No, the real gift of that moment was the gift we gave each other.

The gift of angel wings.

In different religions and traditions, angels are assigned different roles. Some are protectors. Some are messengers. Some are guides. Some are meant to carry out God's tasks.

But think about it—every single one of these angelic functions is something that we, as human beings, are more than capable of.

The dictionary definition of an angel is "a spiritual being believed to act as an attendant, agent, or messenger of God, conventionally represented in human form with wings and a long robe." So—take away the wings and the long robe (at least for me; I don't own one), and that definition can apply to all of us.

We can be one another's protectors, and messengers, and guides. And we can carry out God's tasks—charity, compassion, forgiveness, assistance, and love.

We can be the angels we so desperately need in our lives.

This is not some idle theory I've cooked up. It's not some kind of wishy-washy spiritualism. The existence of angels on earth is real—very, very real. I have seen them, and met them, and heard their stories. I have experienced the powerful impact they can have.

I have seen them work *miracles*.

You may not be able to see their beautiful, feathery wings.

But you will know when one of these angels comes into your life.

After *An Invisible Thread* was published, hundreds of people were inspired to share their own "invisible thread" stories with me. The constant theme of all the letters and stories was that these people hadn't even recognized how meaningful certain moments and gestures had been in their lives. They didn't have a name for the unlikely connection they forged with someone unexpected.

But then, thanks to the story of Maurice and me, they were able to look back at their own moments and gestures and see them for what they were—huge turning points that altered the course of their life's path. And they found a name for their own powerful connections: these were invisible threads.

Most important, it was as if they were finally able to recognize and appreciate the incredible power they possessed—the power we *all* possess—to change the world simply by sharing our innate goodness as human beings.

As angels on earth.

Just imagine how it made me feel to hear from all these people. When I wrote my book, I had no idea what to expect. I just sent it out into the world and waited to see what would happen. Then I began receiving letters and emails from people across the country and around the world, thanking me for sharing my story and telling me how much it meant to them. People thanked me for helping give a name to a special relationship in their lives. People read the book and re-bonded with old invisible thread connections. People were inspired to go out and discover new ones.

This is when I began to understand that the story of Maurice and me wasn't just about the two of us.

It was about the deep, spiritual longing *all* of us have for meaningful, authentic connections in our lives.

What followed for me, in the five years since *An Invisible Thread* came out, was a remarkable journey that helped me develop a brand-new way of looking at life and love and friendships and, yes, angels.

The starting point of my journey was a recognition of the invisible threads that connect us all. But over time, I realized these threads were only a part of a bigger, more powerful equation. Because what truly matters is that we *honor* these connections—and the way we honor them is through kindness. It is a simple yet beautiful model, and it is built on three basic truths:

1. Everyone has invisible thread connections in their lives.
2. We honor and activate these connections through kindness.
3. Honoring our invisible thread connections makes us angels on earth.

You will see that I didn't have to overhaul my life, or even make any radical changes, in order to experience the great blessings of this new view of the world. All that changed was my *perception* of how the world works—my way of thinking about everyday events. About what truly matters in our lives, and what doesn't. About how we all fit into the great, big tapestry of existence.

And that change in perception has changed everything else in my life.

Now, that change didn't happen overnight. It happened over the course of the five-year journey that followed *An Invisible Thread*.

About two weeks after the book was released, I received a phone call from Vicki Sokolik, the founder and executive director of an amazing organization in Tampa called Starting Right, Now. Vicki has taken countless high school students under her wing and been like a mother to them. She sets up each teen with a dedicated mentor, and together they help the students find jobs and housing and deal with school and life issues. On top of all that, Vicki gives the students her unconditional love and support. As a result, these teens have thrived, breaking generational cycles of poverty and homelessness.

Vicki told me her charity was hosting a big event in October 2012, and she asked if I would come and give a speech about my story. I immediately thought, "Are you sure you have the right person?" It had never dawned on me that I'd be invited to talk about my story in front of groups of people.

Honestly, my whole life, I have been terrified of getting up and speaking in front of large crowds. In grade school I stayed away from plays, where I would have to talk, and settled for dance recitals. For a dance recital in the second grade, there was just me and another little girl dancing to "Oh, My Darlin' Clementine." I was terrified and tried to make myself faint, so I wouldn't have to do it. A few grades later, every student had to read the day's announcement over the school loudspeaker. When it was my turn, I went up to the microphone, froze after the first few words, turned around, and walked away in tears. Thankfully, the principal excused me from the announcement.

This wasn't just stage fright. I absolutely dreaded the idea of speaking in front of large groups of people. Later on, when I became an ad sales executive for media companies like Time Inc. and Condé Nast, I worked hard to be able to address small gatherings of clients and colleagues—my comfort level was no more than ten or twenty. But any group larger than that was still a nightmare for me. When I had to deliver an important presentation to fifty coworkers in a big conference room, I stressed out about it for *weeks*.

So naturally, after *An Invisible Thread* came out, what was next for me?

Public speaking.

My first speaking event was at St. John's Episcopal Church in Ivyland, Pennsylvania. I drove two hours and somehow managed to stay on my feet as I shared the story of Maurice and me with the thirty or so people who turned out.

But then the crowds started growing.

I was invited to speak at the Greater Houston Conference for Women, in front of hundreds of people. I told my story at a School Nutrition Association Conference in front of five thousand attendees. I was asked to participate in a global conference called Leadercast Live, which took place in an arena in Atlanta's Gwinnett Center in front of eight thousand people—and was simulcast to 120,000 others around the world.

At that event, I was one of the main speakers, and *I had to follow Archbishop Desmond Tutu!*

I wound up traveling all over the country, from Boston to Hawaii, sharing the story of *An Invisible Thread*. In all, I've given more than one hundred fifty speeches, at corporate functions and charity events, in churches and synagogues, in front of local book club get-togethers. I have also been asked to speak in many elementary schools, middle schools, high schools, and universities, and I found that students of all ages were a huge audience for the message of my book. Through all these events, I have met thousands of people, and I've had hundreds of one-on-one conversations about a subject that was becoming the theme of my speeches and, indeed, my life.

Kindness.

And what I heard over and over, everywhere I went, was this: "The world needs more stories like yours."

Followed, often, by just such a story.

That is how this book was born—in conversations with people

from all different walks of life. In the incredibly heartwarming letters and emails I received from readers around the world, and in the inspirational stories they shared. In the realization that there was a simple, powerful message common to all these stories: that to live our best, happiest, most fulfilling lives, we need to open our eyes and our hearts to the invisible thread connections that are all around us—and we need to *honor and activate* these connections, so we can become angels on earth.

The chance to share some of the stories I've heard with you— and to introduce you to some of the extraordinary people I've met—is one of the best gifts to come out of my five-year journey around the country. The woman who saved a life just by buying a book; the man who made an incredible sacrifice for a total stranger; the boy who found his miracle while selling tacos in a dangerous neighborhood—I simply can't *wait* for you to meet these people.

All the stories in this book came to me through meetings, emails, and conversations; most of them have never been told in print before.

I'm also sharing the insight of some truly remarkable thinkers who crossed my path—people who made subtle shifts in their perception of the world and who beautifully articulate how you, too, can change your life with a simple change of attitude.

As you'll see, I've arranged the stories into seven parts: Kindness, Yesness, Outwardness, Awareness, Uniqueness, Clearness, and Connectedness. I found that different stories spoke to me in different ways and taught me different things about invisible threads and angels. Some stories taught me smaller truths, others taught me really big truths, and all of them put together changed the way I look at the world. These seven parts represent a kind of blueprint of my journey—the step-by-step path I took to a new understanding of why we're here.

The opportunity to share all of this with you now is the continuation of the miracle that started when I met Maurice on a busy street corner thirty years ago. And I hope that when you read these stories, you will react the way I did—with joy and wonder and amazement and hope.

Of course, all of us already have important people in our lives. People we love, people we work with, people we run into while walking our dogs. Relatives, friends, spouses, confidantes. These connections are the very fabric of our lives—they give shape to who we are. And we all try our hardest never to take these connections for granted.

But sometimes we do. Sometimes we get lost in the routines and schedules of everyday life. We allow our world to get too narrow—we draw the circle tighter and tighter around us. Bit by bit, our focus turns inward—and all of a sudden we stop looking outward altogether.

And in this way we miss potential connections that could lead us to our best and happiest selves.

I know this happens, because it happened to me.

When I walked past Maurice on 56th Street all those years ago, my focus was as narrow as it could be. I was turned completely inward, busy with my job and my overscheduled life. There was no time in my hectic days for genuine gratitude and no room for someone like Maurice. And so I kept walking.

I almost failed to see the angel in Maurice.

I know now that there are millions of Laura's and Maurice's out there—people brought together by strange and wonderful circumstances; people bound forever across oceans and decades; people who, through the power of an invisible thread, became angels on earth.

This book is a collection of stories about some of them. And as you read them, be on the lookout for the turning point in all of them—that tiny moment when a simple gesture, a simple act of kindness, changes everything.

That's all this book is—a challenge to you to recognize, and honor, the invisible thread connections in your life, and a guide to appreciating the ways you can be an angel on earth.

The philosopher Seneca once said, "Wherever there is a human being, there is an opportunity for kindness." My journey has taught me that this is true.

But it has also taught me that wherever there is a human being, there is a potential angel on earth. None of us can become angels on our own—it is the *interaction* between two people that creates angel wings.

What I hope more than anything is that, with the stories and inspiration in this book, you will tap into the transcendent power of people being angels for one another.

PART ONE
KINDNESS

Kindness is simple. Kindness is easy. It doesn't take a lot of effort, or even thought. Sometimes it happens automatically, because most humans are, by nature, kind. Don't think of kindness as something you have to do—think of it as something you have to *allow to happen*. These stories taught me that amazing acts of kindness can emerge from the most ordinary events.

1

THE HUG

Dru Sanchez is a mother who lives in Tucson, Arizona, and works at a local newspaper there. One day, she drove to a supermarket near her office to grab something to eat at work. As she walked down an aisle, she noticed a family picking out groceries.

The mom, who was in her twenties, was pushing a shopping cart. Her young daughter, maybe three years old, rode in the cart, and two boys, probably six and eight, walked alongside. The boys were helping their mom put items in the cart. They looked like any other family, and Dru walked past them without a word.

A few minutes later, she saw the family again in a different aisle. This time, she noticed the elder boy holding something in his hands.

A small calculator.

The boy was adding up the price of items his mother wished to buy. Dru glanced into their cart and saw that there were no big boxes of cereal, no six-packs of soda, no packages of cookies. Just a few basics—bread, milk, butter, eggs. In that instant, something remarkable happened to Dru.

"The only way I can describe it is that I felt a strong tug on my heart," she says. "Something was pulling on my heart, and it was telling me, 'You need to do something for this family.'"

But why? Why did Dru have such a strong emotional reaction?

"Because I understood who this mother was," she says. "She was me."

⁓

Twenty years earlier, Dru had been the struggling single mother of two children. Her ex-husband didn't provide any support, so it was up to Dru to do everything for her kids—feed them, bathe them, clothe them, get them to day care, deal with their problems—all while working full-time at the *Los Angeles Times*, first as a clerk and later as a sales manager. She had to drive up to ninety minutes each way to get to work, which left her even less time to be with her children.

"It was a real struggle," she says now. "I was lucky that I had a good job, but there were times when I had to hustle the kids into an after-school or day care program, and then I'd pick them up and have to tell the people I couldn't afford to pay them. They always let me go, and I always promised to pay it forward."

Many times, Dru went shopping with her kids. She didn't use a calculator, but she had to be careful about what went into her cart. Even so, her children always got what they needed, and sometimes even what they wanted.

Twenty years later, in that supermarket in Tucson, she saw her younger self in the mother with three children.

"I could tell this was a family just trying to survive," Dru says. "I knew these children weren't going to get all the food they needed, and I knew their mother knew it, too. And I imagined how heartbreaking that must have been for her."

Still, Dru passed the family by and went to another aisle.

A few minutes later, she ran into them *again* in a different aisle.

"That was God telling me, 'Okay, here's your chance,'" she

says. "It was God saying, 'You're going to do this, and you're going to do it now.'"

Slowly, Dru approached the family. When she had been a struggling single mother herself, Dru never asked anyone for help and probably wouldn't have accepted it had it been offered. Now, she understood this mother might feel the same way.

"Excuse me," Dru finally said. "I don't mean to offend you at all, but . . . I would like to buy your groceries."

Dru braced for what could have been an embarrassing moment. But it never came. Instead, the mother looked at Dru and started crying.

"Really?" the mother asked.

"Yes, yes," Dru said, suddenly wiping tears from her own eyes. "You finish your shopping, and I will meet you up front."

Then Dru quickly walked away. She didn't want anyone else in the store to see what she was doing. She stood near the cash registers and waited patiently for the family to finish shopping and come up.

Five minutes passed. Then ten. Then fifteen.

The family never came up.

Dru worried that she had offended the mother, that she was too proud to let someone pay for her groceries. Maybe they'd even sneaked out a side exit.

Dru went to one of the cashiers and bought a one hundred-dollar gift certificate. Then she went looking for the family.

She found them in the produce section. Before the mother could say anything, Dru handed her the gift card.

"I don't want to make you rush," Dru said. "I just want to give you this. Please take it. That's all."

The mother took the gift card, looked at Dru, and raised her arms. Then she leaned in and hugged Dru tightly. Dru hugged back.

"It was overwhelming," Dru says. "We were both crying like babies."

Finally Dru pulled back and walked away. She wanted to give the family some privacy. She walked a few steps, then heard a voice.

"Wait."

Dru turned around and saw the woman's two boys running right at her. When they got to her, they jumped up and wrapped their arms around her. They held her and hugged her and said "thank you" over and over. Their mother hadn't told them to do it. They just did it. Dru tried to keep it together, but she couldn't.

"I just broke out sobbing," she says. "The boys hugging me was a feeling unlike anything I'd ever felt in my life. I understood the moment between the mother and me. But I didn't expect the kids to hug me. I didn't expect them to feel the same emotion. And they did! They felt the same thing in their hearts that I felt! It was unbelievable."

Dru finally left the store and went back to work, still sobbing. She didn't tell anyone about what happened, but she couldn't stop thinking about it herself. "It was this profound moment for me," she explains. "In that moment, it was as if I learned what life was really about."

Dru returned to the supermarket a few times, hoping to see the family again. But she never did. Still, she now looked at all the shoppers differently. She looked at *everyone* differently. Her eyes were open in a way they'd never been before. "I am always on the lookout now for a situation to do something positive," she says. "That one hug infused me with something really powerful, and I don't think it's ever going away."

Dru knew the gift card wouldn't change that family's life. All it could do was maybe take some pressure off the mother and make her struggle a tiny bit easier. Then again, she realized, that's all it *had* to do.

"It is about trying to give someone what they need *at that moment*," Dru says. "That was my only thought. 'Can I give this woman a little breather? Can I help her just a little at this moment?' I realized that God puts us in each other's paths just for this reason—so that we can help each other in big ways and small ways, too."

Today, Dru still has her eyes open for ways she can help. In line at supermarkets, she's always watching to see if someone can't afford their groceries. Then she offers to help—sometimes fifteen cents, sometimes fifteen dollars. And every time it happens, it fills her with joy and gratitude. "Those feelings are irreplaceable," she says. "They make you understand your place in a difficult world. I may never see that family again, but I'll always remember that moment, and I think they will, too. I'd like to think that when the children grow up, they will do the same thing for others."

One hundred dollars and a hug. That's all that was exchanged. But the exchange itself created something far bigger, far more powerful, far more lasting.

"Sometimes," says Dru, "we just have to let someone know we care about them."

ELEVATION

How can something as simple as a gift card turn a human being into an angel on earth?

It's because kindness elevates.

Kindness elevates the simplest moment into something much bigger. Kindness also elevates us by enhancing our level of connection to the world. In practical terms, acts of kindness have been shown to elevate the levels of dopamine in our brains, producing an enhancement in our feelings of happiness and well-being.

Beyond this, however, I have seen how kindness has a transcendent power. Kindness enlarges everything it touches. Small actions become big actions; tiny moments become turning points; humans become angels. The sum is much greater than the parts.

When it comes to kindness, it's as if there's a lovely, strange magic at work.

2

THE GARAGE DOOR

Laura Lahey Chambers met her husband, Russ, at a friend's wedding. She was the bridesmaid, Russ the best man. That was thirty-five years ago, and they've been together ever since. They have two beautiful children, Josh and Emily, and an awesome son-in-law, Adam, and grandson, Ben. They live a busy, comfortable life in North Canton, Ohio. They are, like me, blessed.

Ten years ago, when Laura's youngest child went away to college, she found she really missed having someone around to fuss over. "All of a sudden I had no kids at home, but I wasn't ready to stop being a mother," she says. "I don't think I ever will be." She felt she still had a lot to offer—guidance, attention, wisdom—so she signed up to volunteer after work with an inner-city school reading program in Canton.

That's where she met Felice.

Laura was paired up with Felice in the reading program, when Felice was seven years old. "She was this funny, hyper, silly, absolutely adorable but also mischievous little girl," Laura says. "Just jumping up and down and dancing and laughing and giggling all the time. A *lot* of energy." Laura didn't know much about Felice's situation, but even so she felt as if they were a good match. "I had this instant understanding about her, and a thought popped into my head: 'She needs me,'" Laura recalls. "At the same time, I knew I needed her, too."

After two reading sessions together, Laura took a chance and called Felice's mother. She wanted to ask permission to take Felice out for ice cream. "I knew she always came to school hungry, and the free meal she got there might have been the only meal she ate all day," Laura says. "I was told she was one of those kids who ate every last vegetable off her plate, because she was hungrier than most."

Laura finally connected with Felice's mother and asked permission for the after-school outing. "Come and take her," was the mother's reply.

Laura drove to where Felice lived, in one of the poorest sections of the city. As soon as she walked into the small, run-down apartment, Felice ran up and hugged her.

"Can we go now? Please?" Felice said.

Then Laura noticed another little girl in the apartment—Felice's sister, Lucy, two years younger.

"Just as I got ready to leave with Felice, Lucy started bawling," Laura says. "She was saying, '"I want to go! Felice can't go without me! I want to go, too!'"

The girls' mother told Lucy to be quiet. "This lady doesn't want to take you," she scolded. Laura bent down to the girl's eye level and said, "If your mother says it's okay, you can come, too."

"Take 'em both," their mother said.

"It was obvious their mom was going through some very hard times," Laura says. "I realized how little this family had, and how little these sisters had been exposed to in their lives. It broke my heart."

Laura piled the girls into her SUV and buckled them into the backseat. "Right away they were marveling at the car," says Laura. "They were amazed by it. So they sat there, their little legs swinging in the air, laughing and giggling about the car."

Laura turned on the radio, and music filled the air. "Now they really couldn't believe it," says Laura. "They'd never been in a car that played music."

Laura drove them to McDonald's and got them everything they wanted. The girls ate a lot of food, and quickly. "But what really got them were the cup holders in the back of the SUV," says Laura. "I know it sounds like nothing, but they were so tickled that they each got a cup holder to put their drinks in. And Felice was like, 'Okay, this is *your* cup holder, and this is *my* cup holder.' They were just so happy about it."

The next stop was Laura's house, where she planned to play a few games with the girls before driving them back home. Laura pulled into her driveway and pressed the garage door remote. The garage door began to rise up.

"And all of a sudden, I just heard the loudest laughter," Laura says. She couldn't understand what was so funny, but finally figured it out.

It was the garage door opener.

"They just could not believe I could click a button and the door would open by itself. They laughed so hard when they saw me do it, and they asked me to do it again."

So Laura lowered and raised the garage door once more.

The girls laughed even louder.

Then Laura said, "Do you want to try?" and handed the remote back to Felice.

Felice carefully held the remote and delicately pressed a button. She watched with wide eyes as the garage door slowly lowered. She pushed it again and watched the door go up. Then it was Lucy's turn. Then Felice's. Then Lucy's again. All the while, the laughter never stopped. It only grew louder.

The three of them sat in Laura's car in the driveway for the next twenty minutes, watching in wonder as the garage door rattled up and down.

Laura became a mentor to the sisters and watched over them for the next eleven years. They lived with her during summers and went along on family trips. She bought them clothes, Christmas presents, and books; she taught them how to swim and read and cook. "Their favorite thing was when I bought them matching outfits," says Laura. "They wore them every Christmas when we went to see *The Nutcracker*."

There were a million other things she did for the girls—got them their first bikes, their first pretty shoes, their first leotards for gym lessons—but mainly what Laura gave them was her time and attention. "It was never about the material things," she says now. "It was the moments. The experiences. It was about *life*! All these little things we take for granted meant the world to these two little girls."

When Felice turned eighteen, she began spending less time with Laura. Lucy soon followed. Inevitably, Laura and the sisters grew apart. "Our relationship had never been an official relationship," Laura says. "It just sort of happened over time. And when it ended, it was difficult. I watched the girls drift away from me, and there was nothing I could do."

Laura would hear reports about how the girls were doing, and those reports weren't always good. They were rebellious teenagers, and sometimes they got into trouble. Once in a while,

Laura would text Felice just to say hi. "I'd write, 'I love you a whole bunch,' and she'd write back, 'Yeah, yeah, love you, too.' Sometimes she wouldn't text back at all." Right now, it's hard to measure what sort of impact Laura has had on the girls, or if it will end up making a difference in their lives. The story of their invisible thread, Laura realizes, "isn't finished yet. There are more chapters to be written. And who knows what the ending will be?"

But no matter what happens with the girls going forward, Laura appreciates what a great gift they've been in her life. "Through all my time with them, I just had this beautiful peacefulness about it," Laura says. "It just felt right to me. Other people might have wondered what I was doing or felt I was crossing a line, but I wasn't focused on that. My only focus was on the girls. 'They need me. We need each other.' That's all I was thinking about. 'We need each other.'"

Few things are certain in anyone's life, but Laura is absolutely certain of one thing: "The invisible thread between us will never, ever be broken. I just know that deep in my heart. I know if I called those girls right now and said, 'Hey, you nutheads wanna get something to eat?' they'd say yes. They would come. That's how strong our connection is."

Recently, Laura put her theory to the test.

She called Felice and asked if she and her sister wanted to go to Friendly's, their favorite restaurant. "Immediately, she said yes," Laura says. "And as soon as I picked them up and they hopped in my car, there was a transformation. We were laughing and giggling and goofing around just as we always had. It was as if nothing had changed."

An unbreakable bond, a lifelong bond, a *forever* bond—and it all began in a driveway, with a garage door that wouldn't stay still.

"Even today, every single time I use the garage door opener, I think about Felice and Lucy, and my stomach does a flip," Laura says. "That was the moment when the girls took over my heart. It was this tiny, simple, insignificant thing, but to the three of us it was so powerful. It was *magic*."

RIPPLES

Not too long after An Invisible Thread came out, I received an email from Talia Bardash, an eleventh grader at the Frisch School in New Jersey.

Talia had read the book and made it the subject of an outside reading assignment that was part of a Twitter project. "I hope I have the strength to be as unselfish as you," she wrote to me in her email. Then she asked if she could interview me for her project, since interviewing an author pretty much guaranteed she'd get an A.

Unfortunately, I was traveling and didn't get home in time to help her with the project. But I promised to make it up to Talia by visiting her school and giving a speech there. My only condition was that Talia had to be the one to introduce me.

On the day of the speech, I finally met Talia, and she was wonderful. Bright, smart, poised—exactly what I expected. Her parents and grandmother were there, too, and they watched proudly as Talia walked onto the stage and talked about An Invisible Thread. When she was done, she came off the stage and sat with her parents. I noticed that her father, Jody Bardash, had tears in his eyes.

After my speech, Talia's father came up to thank me.

"You have made a real difference in my daughter's life," he said. "She wondered if you would keep your word and come to her school, and she couldn't wait to meet you. Thank you for what you have done for her. I would very much like to pay it forward."

He even had an idea for how to do it.

Talia's father was a highly successful dentist who traveled the world helping those who couldn't afford dental services. When he watched a video of Maurice and me, he noticed Maurice's front tooth was badly chipped. He offered to fix the tooth for free.

"I want to give Maurice his beautiful smile back," Dr. Bardash said. And so he did.

I'll never forget the day Maurice texted me a photo of his new front tooth. I don't think I've ever seen him smiling quite that wide.

Getting to meet Talia and her parents, and having Dr. Bardash turn around and do something so special for Maurice, are some of the very best moments of my entire journey, which I will always cherish.

But Talia also taught me something remarkable about angels on earth.

She taught me that every act of kindness has a knock-on effect. Every act of kindness produces a second act of kindness.

We might not always notice it—and it might not be as obvious as Maurice's gleaming new tooth—but it happens somewhere, to someone. That's because kindness is contagious. Kindness leads to more kindness.

Kindness ripples.

It's as if the universe matches every act of kindness with a kind act of its own.

3

THE WALLET

I have a friend, Chuck Posternak, who years ago shared an amazing story with me. It was about a wallet. At the time, I was really moved by his story, but over the years Chuck and I lost touch, and I forgot all about it.

Then my book was published, and Chuck wrote to say hello. He also reminded me of the wallet story. I felt the same emotions all over again, and I asked him if I could share his story in this book.

It started when Chuck was a boy who loved summer camp. He loved it as a camper, and then he loved it even more as a counselor. "There was something about being able to help kids and steer them and watch them develop certain values," Chuck, a highly successful investment executive, says now. "I knew that when I finally left the camp, I wanted to find an extension of that and keep doing it."

What he found was Big Brothers Big Sisters, the century-old nonprofit group that matches vulnerable youngsters with older mentors.

Chuck became a "Big" to a twelve-year-old boy named Lonnie, who lived with his mother and four brothers—but no father—in a small apartment in the dangerous neighborhood of Crotona Park, in the Bronx. "I was only twenty-three, and the first time I went to visit Lonnie at his apartment he walked *me* to the subway because he was worried about *me*," Chuck says. "It was definitely a rough place." During their first year together, Chuck invited Lonnie to go with him on a weekend trip to Massachusetts. Lonnie arrived at the airport with his clothes in a cardboard box, because his family couldn't afford a suitcase.

Chuck was Lonnie's mentor for five full years. In that time they went to New York Knicks and Rangers games, saw lots of movies, made pizza in Chuck's New York City apartment, and sometimes just hung out. Chuck even attended Lonnie's bar mitzvah at a community center in Pelham Parkway. After their Big Brother mentorship officially ended, they stayed in touch but, inevitably, began to drift apart. "I guess I hoped that I'd shown him different directions, different dreams," says Chuck. "But the truth is, I got much more out of my relationship with Lonnie than he did. He was my friend."

In the end, Lonnie did just fine. He now owns an insurance agency and is married with children. "When I went to see him one day after he got married, he was driving a better car than I was," Chuck says with laugh.

What's more, Lonnie never forgot the way his Big Brother changed his life, and so he became a "Big," too. In 2004, at an event marking the hundredth anniversary of Big Brothers Big Sisters, Chuck and Lonnie and Lonnie's mentee, Jake, all got together to tell their story—the story of three generations of lives altered by kindness and love.

"The day we met my life changed dramatically, in ways you can only imagine," Lonnie wrote to Chuck recently. "I consider you my true friend."

⁓

The second part of Chuck's story starts in a taxicab.

It was an ordinary weekday, and Chuck was on his way from

his office to a meeting in midtown Manhattan. He hailed a cab and jumped in the backseat.

And there, he saw the wallet.

"Just a regular brown wallet," he says. "I looked through it, and there were several hundred dollars in it and all these credit cards with the guy's name on them."

Chuck didn't own a cell phone back then, so he found a pay phone and began the process of trying to track down the wallet's owner. It took a few calls, but with his secretary's help, he finally connected with the man and agreed to meet in Grand Central Station, so Chuck could hand over the wallet. Chuck waited at the base of the big clock in the grand foyer—a famous meeting place for a million friends and strangers. But there was no sign of the other guy. Chuck kept circling the clock, walking round and round, but still, nothing.

It turned out the wallet's owner—John Scardino—had been there all along and was doing the same thing: circling the clock, looking for Chuck. "It took us a while, but we finally met," says Chuck. "And he was very appreciative."

To show his thanks, John offered Chuck two tickets to the taping of a popular cooking show featuring Emeril Lagasse. It was a nice gesture, but Chuck politely turned it down.

"I said, 'If you really want to do something for me, let me tell you about this program I'm part of,'" Chuck recalls. "And I went into my standard three-minute speech about Big Brothers Big Sisters. I was always giving people that speech and hitting them up for help." In fact, Chuck loved Big Brothers so much, he became part of its advisory council, then chairman of the council, then the youngest board member in the group's history, and eventually a guiding force on its executive and investment committees.

John listened to Chuck's pitch, thanked him again, and vanished into the crowd of commuters. Chuck had no idea if he'd ever see him or hear from him again. After all, he had found someone else's wallet just a few weeks before and had returned it with no fanfare and no thank you gift. He put the meeting with John out of his head and got on with his life.

What Chuck didn't know was that John Scardino—a successful real estate developer in California—had lost his mother when he was eleven and had basically been forced to fend for himself while his father was busy with work. John lived in an area of Southern California that was riddled with violent gangs, and he had desperately needed a safe place to be a normal kid.

He found it at the Boys Club of Santa Monica. After going to college and law school, he became a big financial supporter of several charities that catered to underprivileged children. John had a deep and heartfelt connection to vulnerable children—the very same connection Chuck had.

One day in 2004, he flew to New York City for a business meeting and dropped his wallet in the back of a taxicab. When he realized he had no ID and couldn't get into the office building for his meeting, he went scrambling down Madison Avenue, chasing cabs and looking into their backseats. But no luck—his wallet was gone.

To his great relief, an hour or so later he heard from Chuck. They met in Grand Central Station, and later that day John flew home to California.

Three weeks later, he called Chuck at his office.

"He told me he was coming back to New York, and he wanted to see me," says Chuck. "We agreed to meet at a Big Brothers Big Sisters fund-raising event in the city."

At the event, John presented Chuck and Big Brothers with a check for ten thousand dollars.

"He said he wanted to thank me by giving this donation," Chuck recalls.

But that wasn't all. John promised to make the same donation every year for the next three years.

"I was blown away," Chuck says. "I got emotional. I was very moved by his generosity. That was forty thousand dollars that otherwise wouldn't have come in. I knew that was going to help a *lot* of children."

Then some newspapers picked up the story of Chuck and John and the wallet, which led to even *more* unexpected contributions to Big Brothers Big Sisters. "I would get calls from people I hadn't heard from in years," says Chuck. "It was amazing. We got a lot of anonymous contributions, too. All that money helped *so* many kids."

And all because of a wallet that had been left in the back of a cab.

"I really don't see that as an accident," Chuck says now. "I mean, two men with the same interest in helping kids? In a city of millions of people? To me, finding that wallet was really a little miracle."

THINK SMALL

Earlier, I mentioned that you don't have to uproot your life, or even do anything especially dramatic, to get started on your journey to seeing the world differently. I've learned that something as simple as a hug can be the catalyst to remarkable change. Even the tiniest demonstration of love, the smallest display of kindness, can have heart-busting, life-changing consequences, both for the ones who show love and the ones who receive it.

So—think small.

Give it a try. Maybe start by saying "hello."

Saying "hello" or "thank you" is the easiest way you can honor your connection to another human being. And the easiest people to say hello or thank you to are the people who cross our paths most often: our neighbors.

Unless you live on a mountaintop or on a boat in the middle of the ocean, you have neighbors. We all have neighbors. These are the people connected to us through geography—the couple next door, the family down the street, that nice man or woman around the corner. But I'm not just talking about people we live next to—I'm talking about people who are our neighbors in life. Grocery baggers, salespeople, gas pump operators, our favorite waiter—everyone who is part of the fabric of our everyday existence.

We say hello to our neighbors all the time. But sometimes, as with many things in our lives, we can end up taking our neighbors for granted. Maybe the hello becomes an absentminded nod. Maybe we drive by their houses without so much as a thought about them. Maybe we ride in an elevator with someone and don't even bother looking up.

We forget that while some invisible threads stretch thousands and thousands of miles, others need only stretch the length of a front lawn or an elevator car.

So just experiment with giving a neighbor a heartfelt hello. Think about him or her as a fellow traveler on your journey. Appreciate your simple but meaningful connection to that person. Give it a try, and see what happens.

See how it makes you feel.

Because sometimes, the simple act of appreciating a neighbor can have wonderfully unexpected results.

4

THE NEIGHBOR

Annie McCormick Bonner's father was in the Navy, which meant she moved a lot when she was young. Thirteen times, to be exact. Her community was always changing, and so were her neighbors. But Annie was also one of ten children, so she had plenty of permanent company. "My parents were Mormons and they wanted fourteen kids, but they stopped at ten," Annie says. "I knew I wanted a big family, but not *that* big."

She and her husband, Kevin—they had been part of the same Seattle-based rock band, Mind Over Water, before they married—settled on four children, all boys. Annie's invisible thread story started when the eldest of those four, Peter, was born.

Annie and Kevin were living in the quaint, blue-collar town of Bremerton, an hour-long ferry ride from downtown Seattle, when Peter came along. Kevin was working as an engineer, but Annie quit her job as a logistics coordinator at Amazon to stay home and raise their child. "I wanted to be a stay-at-home mom, but it was an adjustment," she says. "My job had been my identity, and without it, who was I? I realized I really needed to make friends and become part of my community."

The first friend she made was Gale, who had worked with her at Amazon and lived only two blocks away. Then Gale introduced her to her neighbor, a woman named Shirley. "Shirley was eighty-three, and her husband had passed away," Annie says. "But she was lovely and had really interesting stories to tell. She had a spark."

Annie had the strong feeling that she and Shirley ought to be friends. "I just really liked the idea of it," she says. "Inspiration is like that: you know when something is good for you, and you feel happy about it. The idea of being friends with Shirley just had a real *yesness* about it."

Two weeks after Peter was born, Annie brought him over to meet Shirley. "I handed him to her, and she held him the whole time we were there," Annie remembers. "She fed him his bottle and cuddled him as she told me stories about her life." How she'd grown up in the area, how her father had been a logger, how she'd raised her son. How much fun her life had been when she and her husband were young and beautiful.

For Annie, the two or three hours she spent with Shirley were incredibly important. "When you have a baby, you become this person who can't get it together, who doesn't have time to shower, whose whole life becomes about someone spitting up on you. And that was scary. Sometimes I felt like my life was out of control. And Shirley's house became this beautiful, calm place for me. Just having her hold the baby and talk to me was huge."

Shirley invited Annie to come back, and Annie did just that. In the beginning, there was a tiny bit of awkwardness, as there usually is with a new friend. "You both have to figure out, 'Do I have room in my life and in my heart for this person?'" Annie says. But by her third or fourth trip to see Shirley, all the awkwardness was gone. "I knew she would love Peter, and she did. And I felt very loved by her, too. I think she was lonely, so she was happy to have us, but I needed her, too. She had so much to offer, so much love and wisdom. We mattered to each other. Our friendship really mattered."

Shirley had a collection of tiny glass figurines, and they were on just about every table and shelf in her small home. "Not the best house for a toddler," says Annie. So when Peter started crawling and walking around, Shirley "baby-proofed" her house by moving all her breakables to higher shelves. Shirley was on a fixed income, yet she still bought presents for Peter—a red tricycle, a beautiful rocking horse. She was sure to stock plenty of his favorite circus cookies, and she always put his juice in the special rainbow-colored plastic cup she had bought just for him. "Peter adored her," Annie says. "He always knew that he kind of belonged to her, too. When he got old enough to walk, he would run up and hug her. It was always fun for him at Shirley's house."

Before long, Peter was calling Shirley "Grandma." Annie, too, caught herself referring to her friend as Grandma Shirley. "My own grandparents died when I was a child," she says. "I didn't think about that when Shirley and I became friends, but eventually I did. My mother always tells me that a grandmother's love is a very special love. I finally understood what that meant."

As for Shirley, she liked to call Annie's son "my little Peter boy."

"That's what she would always say when she saw him running in," says Annie. "'How's my little Peter boy today?'"

Shirley was always there with a kind word and a cookie through all of Peter's first year, and then his second, and his third, and into his fourth.

Then, one day, Shirley asked Annie the same question several times.

"She couldn't remember what we'd just talked about," Annie says. "She asked me the same thing over and over. She had to take medications, and I worried that she would forget them, too. All of a sudden, I got scared."

━━━✦━━━

Shirley was showing early signs of dementia. It was gradual, but it was worrisome. Annie called Shirley's son, Larry, who lived almost two hundred miles away. "He knew his mother was going to need help someday, and there was a heaviness in his heart when we talked," Annie says. "He didn't want to have to take Shirley's freedom away." At first, Larry hired caretakers to be with his mother every day. But having new people in her house frightened her. She became less joyful and more agitated. Her memory got worse. Both Annie and Larry knew what the next step had to be.

"It wasn't safe for her anymore," Annie says. "She needed to be in a home for older adults. That was always the last resort, but Larry called and we talked it over, and he decided to do it."

The hardest part for Annie was explaining it all to her young son.

"I sat him down and I said, 'Grandma Shirley is going away,'" Annie says. "By then, he knew that she was sick. He knew what was happening. He understood Shirley was going where she would be safe."

On the day Larry came to get his mother, Annie brought Peter over so they could say goodbye. Annie tried to keep her emotions in check, and so did Larry, but it was hard. Shirley's memory had gotten worse, and she didn't even remember she was moving.

"She needs some things to take with her," Larry whispered to Annie. "Can you pack a bag for her?"

So Annie went around the house and gathered a few small items for Shirley—clothes, pajamas, slippers, personal things like that. Everything else, including Shirley's beloved glass figurines, would be packed up later and moved to her new home. The special little basket in which Shirley kept all of Peter's toys, and his rainbow sippy cup, and all the other things she had bought for him over the years—soon they would all be gone, too.

And then it was time for Larry and Shirley to go.

Annie went over and hugged her friend, and held on for a while, and said, "I promise we'll come visit." She tried not to cry, but it was no use. "I felt like we were slicing her heart open by taking her," she says. "It was horrible."

Peter had his chance to say goodbye, too. He bounded over and jumped up and gave Grandma Shirley a big hug and a big kiss. "He was too young to understand the permanence of what was happening," Annie says. "But still, I could tell he was sad."

And then Shirley and Larry got into his car and drove away.

＊＊＊

Every few days, Annie mailed something to Shirley—a letter, a drawing, a little gift. Peter drew colorful pictures for her and scribbled "I miss you" at the bottom. Annie sent Shirley a framed photo of "her little Peter boy" for her desk. She also found a bracelet with tiny little frames attached to it, and she put photos of Peter in the frames and sent the bracelet to Shirley, too. Eventually, Annie and her family drove to visit Shirley in the care facility where she lived. "It was a beautiful place, and she had her own lovely apartment, but my worry was that she wouldn't remember us," Annie says. "And then Peter went in and ran up to her and hugged her, and she hugged him back. She remembered him. She remembered me, too."

A few months later, Annie's cell phone rang. It was Larry calling.

"I want to let you know my mother passed away today," he said softly.

Annie thanked Larry and said goodbye and put her cell phone down. She went into her living room and found Peter playing there. She told him she needed to talk to him, and they sat down together on the sofa.

"I have some sad news," she told him. "Grandma Shirley passed away, and she's in heaven now."

Peter sat silently for a moment, and then he started to cry. Annie kept talking.

"Grandma Shirley isn't sick anymore. She isn't old anymore. She is with all the people she loves now. She is with her husband again."

Then Annie and Peter tried to imagine just what Shirley's life was like in heaven.

"We imagined her in her prime," Annie says. "We imagined her as this young and beautiful woman, with her young and handsome husband. We imagined her surrounded by all their friends from all the wonderful stories she used to tell. We imagined her on this beautiful, happy adventure."

⁓⁓⁓

A few years have passed now, and Peter isn't so "little" anymore. He is fourteen and getting taller every day. "But you know," Annie says, "I still call him 'my little Peter boy.' I'll see him and I'll say, 'How's my little Peter boy today?'"

Every now and then, Annie and Peter will talk about Grandma Shirley and remember the happy times they shared. "He had five years with her," Annie says. "That period was very important for him. Knowing Shirley changed him. It changed all of us."

The great lesson of their friendship, Annie believes, was a lesson we're all taught when we're young: "Love thy neighbor as thyself." "We have these people in these houses right next door to us, and sometimes there is so much potential for love and warmth and wisdom and happiness there," she says. "And all we have to do is look out for that connection."

In other words, all Annie did was make time for a neighbor. Drop in to see a neighbor. Appreciate a connection that was already there. She didn't know where it would lead, but it wound up leading to something beautiful. "Peter and I learned so much from Shirley," she says. "We learned about aging. We learned about friendship. We learned about the importance of remembering. Peter knew that Shirley loved him very much. And he knew her life was better because he loved her."

Most of all, she says, "Peter learned that just by being himself and sharing his time, *he could do something meaningful and important for someone else.*"

That is how Shirley and Peter Boy became angels on earth for each other.

"Long ago, someone told me that it takes five years for an apple seed to become a little tree," Annie wrote in her email to me. "I have often thought that Shirley's effect on me and on Peter is a forever thing. We had five short, precious years together, but maybe that was only the beginning. Maybe we will see this remarkable friendship bearing fruit for generations to come."

PART TWO
YESNESS

Annie Bonner used a word I really love: "yesness." It captures a feeling, a moment, a little internal click of affirmation—a realization of the rightness of something. The stories in this section taught me that angels don't traffic in "no." Angels are in the business of "yes." Our lives become more meaningful if our actions are based on love, not fear—and if, when we feel that internal click, we say yes, not no.

5

THE SNOWSTORM

Imagine being seventeen years old and getting kicked out of your house, with no chance to pack your clothes, no money in your pocket, and no place to go.

In the middle of a blinding snowstorm.

That's what happened to my friend Linda DeCarlo.

Linda and I worked together at *People* magazine back in the 1980s. We liked to go to lunch and talk shop. Sometimes we talked about our families, but mainly we talked about work. We never really dug too deeply into each other's lives—that's not what our relationship was like. But we had a really nice, really easy connection. Then I left for another job, and after that we drifted apart, as colleagues sometimes do.

I hadn't heard from Linda in many, many years when I received an email from her in late 2011. She'd come across *An Invisible Thread* and felt compelled to write to me.

And in her email, which was only three paragraphs long, Linda told me more about herself and who she really was than she ever had in all our lunches together.

In the email, Linda shared an amazing story with a powerful message. I wrote her back and asked if we could talk. I wanted to know more about what happened to her that long-ago night and about the extraordinary act of kindness that helped her come through it alive.

Linda's life was uneventful until she turned five. That's when her father abruptly left the family. Linda's mother, a college-educated school librarian living in Brooklyn, eventually got remarried to a widowed longshoreman who had four kids and a serious drinking problem. Linda's mom and her stepdad, Sal, bought a house together and moved their kids—all seven of them—into the new place.

Almost immediately, her stepdad started trying to get rid of Linda and her two sisters.

"When he drank he got very angry with us, and he always drank," says Linda. "So he began picking us off one by one. My younger sister Nancy was the first to get pushed out. Sal gave my mom an ultimatum. So my mom sent her to live with my dad in California."

Linda's other sister, Sara, was next. "And once she was pushed out," says Linda, "it was my turn." Except Linda's mother didn't want her to go—after all, that would leave her with no children of her own in the house. Sal agreed to let Linda stay, but he never stopped trying to chase her away. "The next few years were sheer torture," says Linda. "He was very creative in the ways he made me miserable."

For starters, Sal forbade Linda's mother from spending any money on her—not a single dime. He went into her room when she wasn't there and threw out some of her clothes. He hid her books and rearranged her room, just to bother her.

"It's my house," he'd tell her. "I can do whatever I want."

Then one cold February day, Sal convinced himself that Linda had stolen something from one of her sisters, who was visiting at the time. Linda denied it, which only made Sal angrier. Finally, he hit her in the face.

Linda hit him back.

"That was one of the best moments of my life," she says now. "I had a lot of pent-up anger."

But the fight was the last straw for Sal. The next day, he marched Linda out of her room and told her she had to leave. No debate, no discussion, no time to pack—just "Go." Linda's mother was crying, but she was powerless to stop what was happening.

"So I went downstairs and took my little ten-speed bike," Linda says, "and walked right out the front door."

And right into the snowstorm.

The winds were howling, and the snow was piling up. The streets were empty, and the few cars on the road were going slowly. It was one of those storms where, if you didn't have a good reason to be outside, you stayed indoors. Except Linda didn't have that choice.

She stood on the sidewalk outside her home and wondered what to do. The only place she could think to go was her friend Cynthia's house, but that was four miles away in Brighton Beach. Still, she had to go somewhere, so Cynthia's house it was. Linda climbed on her bicycle and began pedaling through the snow. It was a long, cold journey, but Linda couldn't stop. She had to keep pushing, keep going.

Finally, three hours later, she was at her friend's front door. With a shivering hand, she knocked three times.

"My stepdad just threw me out," she told Cynthia through sobs. "I have nowhere else to go."

The decision to take her in, of course, wasn't up to Cynthia. It was up to her father, Irving.

A semi-retired widower with four children and not much money, Irving lived in a small, cramped apartment barely big enough for his own family. Why in the world would he ever agree to take in someone else's teenage kid? Linda stood nearly frozen in the foyer, while Cynthia explained the situation to her dad. Finally, Irving came to the door. He looked sternly at the drenched young girl.

Then he put his hand on her shoulder, and he told her something she would never forget.

He said, "You can stay as long as you want."

That was it. Eight words and a hand on her shoulder. But to this day, Linda can summon the intense feeling of relief those eight words produced.

"It was like a lifeline to a drowning girl," she says.

Objectively speaking, it wasn't much of an apartment. It was right beneath the elevated subway, so it was noisy all the time, and it rattled when trains went by. And Irving was so poor he couldn't afford to pay for heat, so in winter it got really cold.

But to Linda, it was home.

Warm, beautiful, wonderful home.

When it was laundry time, Irving's family washed Linda's clothes along with their own. When it was dinnertime, she ate alongside everyone else. When there were outings, she was part of the gang, no questions asked.

"They treated me like I was a member of the family," says Linda. "They never once made me feel like I was some outsider."

Linda wound up staying for a year.

Eventually, she began writing letters to her biological father, whom she barely knew, and wound up moving to California to stay with him. She went to college, got married, had two lovely children, and worked as a financial systems analyst for the same company for more than twenty-five years. Whenever she hit a rough patch, she thought of the lesson Irving always taught her—and that she has since tried to teach her own kids: *We are given small blessings all the time, and we need to learn to appreciate them.*

"Irving would always say that you can't stay upset on a sunny day," Linda says. "That was his philosophy. No matter what was bothering you, if it was sunny outside, and sometimes even when it wasn't, you had to smile." Today, whenever Linda looks out a window and sees a blue sky, she smiles.

When she thinks about getting kicked out at seventeen, Linda realizes things could have gone so much worse for her. She could have fallen in with a bad crowd. She could have ended up on drugs. She might have become homeless. There were many scenarios in which she saw herself dying before she turned twenty-one.

Instead, a bighearted man took her into his home—for a whole year—for no reason other than kindness and decency. And that made all the difference in Linda's life.

"It takes a lot of courage to invest in someone, to take an interest in someone's life," she says. "I am always telling Irving what a beautiful thing he did for me, and every time he just shrugs it off. 'Just pay it forward,' he says."

Not long ago, Linda attended Irving's ninetieth birthday party in his daughter's home in Livingston, New Jersey.

In a corner of the living room, she saw Irving sitting in a chair with his five adult grandchildren huddled around him. She made her way toward him and listened to the story he was telling them.

The story was about her.

Irving described how Linda showed up at his door one snowy night, and how he took her in and made her part of the family.

"And then he told his grandchildren the moral of his story," says Linda. "He said, 'Whenever you have a chance to help someone, you have to do it. *Because that chance is a blessing.*'"

Then someone brought out the birthday cake, and Irving blew out the candles, and Linda went over and gave him a big hug, and Irving hugged his daughter right back.

Irving passed away before the publication of this book. His life was a portrait of kindness and compassion, and he will be missed.

TWO WORLDS

Linda's story helped me understand how opportunities to be angels are all around us all the time. But recognizing them is a matter of perception.

No one would have blamed Irving if he'd decided to drive Linda to a police station, or drop her off at a church, or otherwise funnel her into the system that cares for unwanted kids.

But that's not how Irving perceived the moment. To him, Linda's appearance on his doorstep wasn't an imposition, or a hassle, or a problem to be avoided. To him, Linda's appearance was a chance to say yes.

It all depends on how you see the world. Do you see the world as a cold and random and disconnected place?

Or do you see the world as a place that is rich with connections, relationships, and opportunities to love and share and grow?

More important, which of these two worlds would you rather live in?

6

THE KNOCK

It was an ordinary afternoon in her Southern California home, and LaJuana Moser's three children were playing noisily in the backyard. LaJuana was inside folding laundry when she heard a knock. She opened her front door and didn't see anyone—until she looked down.

There stood a scruffy, sweet-faced four-year-old boy.

"Can I play with your kids?" the boy asked in a quiet voice.

"What?" LaJuana asked, not sure she understood.

"I can hear them in your yard," the boy said. "Can I play with them?"

"Where did you come from?"

"Down the street."

"Where is your mother?"

"Down the street."

"Does she know you're here?"

"Yes."

"Does she know you want to come in?"

"She doesn't care."

LaJuana sized up the situation. She'd seen the child before, riding a bicycle through the streets at 11:00 p.m., and she'd wondered, "He's four—why is he out by himself at night?"

She figured the boy's mother was the woman who lived two houses down—a single mother she knew to have a serious drug problem.

"What's your name?" she asked the boy.

"Jeffrey."

"Jeffrey, do you listen to rules?"

"Yes."

"Good. We have a trampoline in the backyard, so you have to take off your shoes."

"Okay."

"Come on in, then," LaJuana said, and she brought the boy into her home.

LaJuana introduced Jeffrey to her three children—the youngest was nine, the oldest twelve—and sat down to watch them play for a while. Jeffrey laughed as he jumped up and down on the trampoline, trying to go higher each time. Then he hopped on the swing set, and after that he went wading in the swimming pool. The children played together for a long time before Jeffrey finally came back into the house. Then he plopped himself on the sofa and instantly fell fast asleep.

"I let him sleep for as long as he needed," LaJuana says. "I knew his mother was up all night doing drugs, with different people coming and going, and I figured the poor kid never was able to get a good night's sleep. So I let him sleep."

The hours passed, and no one came to ask about Jeffrey. Finally, that night, there was another knock at the door. LaJuana answered it and saw a man she didn't know.

"Is Jeffrey here?" the man asked.

"Yes, he is," LaJuana said.

"Well, his mom just got arrested by six cops," the man said. Then he walked away.

LaJuana kept Jeffrey with her that night. In the morning, she expected someone to come looking for him, but no one did. Later on, LaJuana glanced out her window and saw Jeffrey's mother walking down the street.

"Do you want to go see her?" she asked him.

"No," Jeffrey said.

Eventually, Jeffrey did go back to his mother's house. But the next day, he was back on LaJuana's front porch, knocking on the door again.

"Jeffrey," LaJuana said when she saw him standing there.

"My mom says you gotta watch me," he said.

"Well, okay then," LaJuana said. "Come on in."

That went on for the next three years. Jeffrey would show up at LaJuana's door, sometimes with a note from his mother—"You have to watch him, I have a dentist's appointment"—sometimes not. Over the years the notes piled up in a drawer, most of them unread. "What does it matter what her excuses are?" LaJuana thought. "What matters is that we both understand Jeffrey is our shared responsibility now." And that was okay with LaJuana, because before she ever knew anything about the boy or his situation, the connection between them was already there.

"The second I saw him at my door, I fell in love with him," she says. "And when I learned of his situation, I just made a decision—I'm going to give this kid a safe place in the world. I didn't care about anything else, or how hard it would be, or what trouble I'd be inviting. I just decided—I want him to be safe, and I will be there for him."

In those three years, Jeffrey and his mother were evicted and moved about thirty times. For one stretch, they lived out of a Dumpster in a park. "Jeffrey told me his mother went right to sleep, but he was too scared and it smelled too bad, so he stayed up all night," LaJuana says. Though she couldn't do anything to spare Jeffrey from such horrors—his mother had no intention of giving up custody—LaJuana did what she could to make his life with her as comfortable as possible. She gave him his own bedroom and played soft music that helped him fall asleep (his mother played really loud music all the time). And she filled his room with his favorite toys—Beanie Baby zoo animals. "He had his whole collection lined up next to his bed," she says.

Before meeting LaJuana, Jeffrey had never—not a single time—eaten a meal sitting at a table. Naturally, it took her a while to teach him how to sit still, how to hold a fork and spoon, how to eat with his mouth closed. Nor had he ever had a truly nutritious meal. LaJuana would bring out a plate of something she'd cooked and set it in front of Jeffrey.

"Do I like this?" he'd ask.

"Yes, you do," LaJuana would say.

"Okay. But what is it?"

"Meat loaf and mashed potatoes."

"Okay."

And no matter what it was, Jeffrey always loved it.

LaJuana taught him how to do many things. How to brush his teeth. How to bathe. How to pray. "At four he knew how to roll a joint," she says, "but not much else." When she drove him around to stores and supermarkets, she made a point of showing him pretty things—trees, birds, clouds. "Those weren't the things he'd usually notice," she says. "One of the first times I took him out, he pointed at a man in a car and said, 'That's an undercover FBI agent.'"

She also bought Jeffrey new clothes when he started kinder-garten, and she kept all of his nice things in her home, so they wouldn't get stolen or sold. "I must have replaced his backpack ten times because it kept going missing," she says. But even as she made sure Jeffrey had what he needed, LaJuana also taught him that some children had far less than he did. LaJuana runs a nonprofit called Bags4Kids that helps provide underprivileged children with some basic needs—shoes, clothes, toys, and, yes, backpacks. "Jeffrey helped me pack the backpacks for other kids, and he *loved* helping," LaJuana says. "Not once did he ever say, 'Hey, I don't have anything.' He was happy with what he had. I never bought him anything fancy. But every child deserves a bed and books and clothes."

When Jeffrey's mother finally got a trailer of her own to live in, LaJuana hoped his situation might improve just a little bit. But then one day the police arrived to evict his mother yet again.

"Do you want to go inside and get some of your son's things?" an officer asked Jeffrey's mother.

"No, but can I get the beer in the refrigerator?" she replied.

It was LaJuana who rushed into the trailer to retrieve whatever she could of Jeffrey's few belongings. There were empty booze bottles everywhere. LaJuana saw one of Jeffrey's shoes in a heap of trash on the floor and picked it up. She found another different shoe somewhere else. She took home what she could of Jeffrey's clothes and cleaned them. "But my heart was broken," she says. "It was devastating to see that this was Jeffrey's life."

One day, Jeffrey didn't come knocking on LaJuana's door, as he usually did. The next day passed with no sign of him, either. LaJuana asked around about his mother and learned she'd abruptly skipped town and moved to Las Vegas.

And she'd taken Jeffrey with her.

That was several months ago, and LaJuana hasn't seen Jeffrey since. When she first sent me an email telling me about Jeffrey, he was still with her. Now he's gone, but the connection remains.

When they were together, LaJuana always played a special game with Jeffrey, in which she'd ask him questions about herself. "I'd ask him, 'What's my first name? What's my last name? Where do I live? Where do I work?' And I'd tell him, 'If a social worker ever asks you if you have a grandma, you will tell them, "Yes." And we'd both shout out the word 'YES!' together. And if one day in the future, Jeffrey comes knocking on my door again, I will hug him and bring him right in."

Just because LaJuana has lost touch with the sweet boy who wandered onto her front porch doesn't mean their journey is over. All it means is that it's ongoing. The full story hasn't been written yet. But what struck me most about their story is the incredible miracle of how they found each other.

Jeffrey's mother bounced from place to place, and one of those places happened to be two doors down from LaJuana. What's incredible about that is that LaJuana isn't just an exceedingly kind person. *She is probably the one person who was best equipped to help Jeffrey at that moment.*

LaJuana was adopted herself and raised by parents who had seven kids in all, two of them from Korea. "I grew up in a big melting pot," she recalls. "My dad was a doctor, and he took care of kids who needed taking care of." When LaJuana was little, she started fantasizing about the family she would one day have. "I was very specific about it—I wanted twelve kids," she says. "I wanted them in all different colors."

She got close—as a foster mother she took in as many as seven children at one time, on top of her own three children. "My kids would wake up for breakfast, and there would be someone new sitting at the table," she says. "A lot of times I ended up with kids who were taken out of a dangerous situation and brought to me in the middle of the night."

So on the day that Jeffrey heard the sweet and innocent sound of children playing in a backyard and wandered over to LaJuana's house and knocked on her front door, he found someone who was unusually suited to offering him a safe place in the world.

That is the power of an invisible thread—it connects us to those we can and should be angels for. It draws us together precisely when we need each other most.

And it keeps us connected even after we physically separate.

"All I can do for Jeffrey right now is pray for him," LaJuana says. "But I do think I made a difference in his life. I never set out to take him away from his mother; all I did was let them know that I would be there for Jeffrey no matter what. And that hasn't changed. That will *never* change.

"And I know that someday, I will see Jeffrey again. I know that, because I believe an angel brought him to my door."

BUBBLE PEOPLE

Sometimes opportunities to be angels knock on our front doors, as was the case for Linda and Irving and LaJuana and Jeffrey. But these "knocks" aren't always literal. A knock can be anything that gets our attention. In my case, the knock was three words.

"I am hungry."

That's what I heard Maurice say to me as I passed him on Broadway in 1986. Or rather, that's what my ears picked up. My brain didn't register the words right away, so basically I heard them without really hearing them. That's why I walked passed Maurice on my way to wherever.

But then I stopped in my tracks, because finally the words did register. And they were heartbreaking.

Sometimes, we become bubble people. We walk around inside bubbles of our own making. I should know—I was a bubble person. When I was younger and devoted to building my career in advertising sales, I was way, way inside my bubble. Thankfully, those three words from Maurice popped the bubble.

What I've learned from people like Linda and LaJuana, and from so many others I've met on my journey, is that we cannot live our best lives in a bubble.

Living our best lives means we don't just see, we observe. We don't just hear, we listen. We don't ignore, we engage.

And in this way, the opportunities to be angels that are all around us cease to be hidden and become gloriously apparent.

7

THE BOOKSTORE

A couple of years into my journey, I received an email from a really nice man named Jim Kettlewell.

Jim is the son of a Presbyterian minister, and he grew up in a family that valued community service. He and his wife, Kathy—a onetime classmate; they've been married for forty-four years—have been kind of heart and charitable of mind their whole lives. To hear that such a wonderful person read and enjoyed my book was hugely satisfying.

But what really stood out about Jim's note was his description of the extraordinary event that happened two minutes *after* he finished reading *An Invisible Thread*.

If anyone other than a minister's son had told me this story, I probably wouldn't believe it.

~~~~~~~

The morning of the event, Jim drove to a bookstore not far from his home in a suburb of Canton, Ohio. He'd worked his whole life in the bakery business, but now he was retired, and he loved to read. He was three-quarters of the way through *An Invisible Thread*, and his plan was to finish reading it at the store and buy another book to read next. He went to the store's small café, ordered a coffee (black, no sugar), and settled into a nice, comfortable chair.

It took him about an hour to finish the book.

When he was done, he sat back, closed his eyes, and reflected on my story. He stayed like that for just a minute or two. He opened his eyes and got ready to go, but before he could even get out of his chair, he heard a man talking on a cell phone behind him. "He started talking just as soon as I got ready to go," says Jim. "Another thirty seconds, and I never would have heard him."

He didn't mean to eavesdrop, but he couldn't help it—the man was speaking louder than he should have been. Jim turned and looked him over. The man was in his twenties, and he was trying to keep his voice down but was clearly upset about something. He spoke politely, and with a Southern accent, which made Jim think he was far from home. There were several other people sitting nearby, but no one else paid attention to him. "He knew we were in a reading area, yet he was talking kind of loudly," says Jim. "I didn't think he was being rude. I thought he was in some kind of trouble."

Jim stayed in his chair and listened some more. Gradually, he made sense of the man's story. He learned the man had just received a paycheck for his first two weeks on a new job. The man had deposited the paycheck the day before, but his bank was holding it up until the funds cleared. That, it seemed, was the problem. The man needed money right away.

"He was living in a motel with his daughter, and he was begging the guy at the motel to let him stay another night, even though he couldn't pay for it," says Jim. "I remember hearing him say, 'I only have four dollars in my wallet.'" From what Jim could tell, the motel manager wasn't budging.

The man's next call was to a homeless shelter.

Jim listened as the man called several different homeless shelters, only to be told they were full, or they couldn't take a single man with a child. With every new call, Jim heard the man's voice get more and more desperate. "That's when I started hearing my father's voice in my head, too," says Jim. "My father was a really giving man, and I could hear him saying to me, 'Jim, it's good to have a little money, because sometimes a little money can fix a big problem.' And that's when I knew that I would help this man."

But wait—what if it was a setup? What if it was a scam? The thought crossed Jim's mind, only because of the incredible timing. Could it really have been just a coincidence that he started hearing the man's story *precisely* when he finished reading a book about compassion? "The thing is, I rarely go to bookstores, and I almost never sit down and read there," says Jim. "And then to have this man twelve feet away begin to unravel his story? It was so ridiculous that it *felt* like it just might be a setup."

Yet Jim quickly dismissed that thought. He decided the encounter wasn't a setup. He decided it wasn't a coincidence, either. He decided it was something else. "It was like the divine fates had this plan for me," he says.

Jim is a man who is used to relying on his gut instincts and his faith. So in the bookstore, he relied on them once again. He watched as the man finished his final call, crossed something out in a notebook, and put his head in his hands. It was time for Jim to act.

"Young man," Jim called out.

At first he didn't hear him.

"Young man," Jim said louder.

Finally, the man looked up. Jim motioned with his hand for him to come over. Slowly, the man got up and sat down next to Jim.

"I heard what you were going through," Jim said. "You have a problem. Now let's figure out how to fix it."

Whatever suspicions Jim might have had about the man disappeared as soon as he sat down. "It was just a feeling," he says. "I knew he was for real." At the same time, the man showed no fear of Jim, no hesitation, no skepticism about his motives. It was as if there was something unspoken between them right from the start. "I told him my name was Jim, and he told me his was Rick, and that was it—no last names," Jim says. "I said, 'Let's go,' and we got up and walked out."

Outside the store, Jim learned more of Rick's story. He was working as an electrical apprentice on a construction site at a nearby university, and his boss had let him take time off so he could handle a personal situation. The personal situation was figuring out where he was going to sleep that night. He'd come up to Akron with his daughter, who was three, and found a day care for her so he could go to work. But then his paycheck didn't clear, and he ran out of money. The motel was going to kick them out and put all their belongings on the street. Meanwhile, the seven homeless shelters had turned them away, too.

"What about her mother?" Jim asked.

"She's out of the picture," Rick said. He explained that he'd won sole custody of their daughter, but the divorce had cost him all his savings.

"Come with me," Jim told him. "My bank isn't too far from here."

Together they drove in silence to an ATM. There, Jim pulled out three hundred dollars. "I was still hearing my father's voice saying, 'Jim, you can help this guy, you can solve this guy's problem, and it won't really affect you in any way.' And this was true: it was a relatively small amount of money for me. But for Rick, it was everything."

Jim handed the stack of twenty-dollar bills to, essentially, a stranger. Rick counted them and looked up.

"This is too much," he said. "A hundred dollars will do. Even fifty."

"The deal is done," Jim said. "This isn't about me or you; this is the Lord's work. You don't know what you're going to need tomorrow or the next day. You and your daughter have to eat. So just take it."

Sheepishly, the man folded the money and put it in his pocket. Jim drove him to a nearby restaurant, where he could meet up with a coworker and hitch a ride back to the construction site. Before he got out of the car, Rick took out his pen and notebook and asked for Jim's address.

"I promise I will send you the money as soon as I can," he said.

"There's no need," Jim said. "Someday, years from now, you'll be in a position to help someone, and if you're able to do it, just go ahead and do it. That'll be all the repayment I need."

Rick put his pen and notebook away and quickly wiped a tear from his eye. Jim wiped one from his eye, too. "Nothing flowing down our cheeks, nothing like that," says Jim. "I guess we both just welled up a bit. We both knew that we were connected now."

Rick and Jim shook hands across the front seat. Rick got out of the car and waved goodbye, and Jim waved back. Then Rick walked away.

The two men never saw each other again. "This happened about two years ago, but I still think about Rick every day," says Jim. "Sometimes I think about trying to find him, because I'd like to know that things turned out well for him. But, you know, I never have."

Yet just the memory of their encounter still makes Jim emotional. "The timing of it had to be perfect, or else it never would have happened," he says. "I mean, I had just turned the last page of your book, and it's about how one moment in time changed your life and changed Maurice's life, and the very next second the same kind of moment was presented to me. It's baffling. It's almost supernatural."

Yes, there were reasons—good, solid reasons—why Jim should have ignored Rick and gone on with his day. It might have been a scam. It might have even put Jim in a dangerous situation. Any way you look at it, Jim was taking a risk by offering to help a stranger. "I get all that, and there are some situations where I would just walk away," he says. "But there are also some chances that are worth taking."

Mostly, Jim listened to the voice of his father, who had long since passed away. He connected to his family's legacy of goodness and kindness, and he allowed words spoken decades ago to ripple through time and become brand-new, guiding his actions. "Everything had already been laid out for me, by my father, my mother, my Sunday school teachers, lots of people," says Jim. "Everything I'd ever been taught led me to this one moment with a stranger in a bookstore. All I had to do was act."

When Jim wrote to me and shared his story, he was careful to say that he didn't want any credit for what he had done. He told me he considered his actions to be small in nature. "Puny" was the word he used. I understood what he was getting at. No one in this book shared their stories with me because they wanted credit. They shared them in the hope that others would be inspired by them.

Still, even Jim realized he was wrong to call his actions "puny."

"I said my actions were fairly small, but what I've learned is that's not true at all," Jim says. "What I did was help someone who was in need. And when you do that, it is *never* small."

And everything that happened was all because Jim Kettlewell didn't just hear. Jim *listened*.

PURITY OF HEART

People ask why it took me twenty-five years to share the story of Maurice and me. It's because, for a long time, I didn't know if anyone would care.

Even when people began telling me, "You ought to write a book," I still didn't see it. I still thought what happened with Maurice and me—our special friendship—was relevant only to us.

But after I finally wrote the book, and sent it out into the world, and started hearing from so many people who found something meaningful in our story, I saw how wrong I was. The more people I met and the more stories I heard, the more I began to accept a new reality—that I lived in a world filled with invisible thread connections. My view of existence was changing.

I realized I was on a spiritual journey, a journey to understand myself—and my place in the world—better.

One of the biggest lessons of that journey was taught to me by children.

After An Invisible Thread came out, I heard from a lot of teachers and administrators who wanted me to come to their schools and talk to their students. I'd never really thought about the appeal or impact of our story on children and teenagers, but I kind of doubted anyone other than adults would be interested. But I was wrong again—young people turned out to be one of my most attentive and passionate audiences.

I remember addressing a group of young children in elementary school. After telling them all about Maurice and me, I asked them, "What do you think a small act of kindness is?"

One boy shot up his hand.

"I guess a small act of kindness is, if you see someone during recess standing by themselves, you can have them come over and play with you so they won't be alone," he said in a soft, hesitant voice.

"Yes!" I said. "That is a wonderful act of kindness, because the child who is alone feels bad not having any friends to play with."

Just then, another little boy in the class—Anthony—raised his hand.

"That happened to me," Anthony said.

"What happened to you, Anthony?"

"I was at recess and nobody wanted to play with me. And it made me feel sad."

I had to pull myself together quickly so I wouldn't cry in front of everyone. But before I could even say anything, another boy in the class spoke up.

"We are never going to let that happen again," he said to Anthony.

"Yeah," another boy said, "you can come join us, too."

"And us, too," said someone else. "You can always play with us."

Needless to say, this spontaneous outpouring of encouragement— the instinctive kindness these children demonstrated—left me breathless.

But it also taught me that there is a beautiful purity to the way youngsters respond to opportunities to be angels. It is a purity of heart.

Because they have fewer defenses built up, they are able to respond more quickly to these opportunities than most of us grown-ups are. When his classmates learned about Anthony's loneliness, they responded to it immediately. They instinctively appreciated their connection to Anthony, and in the same instant they honored it. Now, the many different forces that affect us throughout our lives most likely will muddy that beautiful purity. But what I learned is that it's there, inside us all, and that if we try, we can summon it again.

And when we do, we can more easily recognize and seize the opportunities that are out there to be angels.

8

THE MITZVAH

In 2013, I received an email from an eleven-year-old sixth grader named Avital.

Avital explained that her school—Ezra Academy, in Woodbridge, Connecticut—had assigned her a project: she had to write about her modern-day mitzvah hero. *Mitzvah* is a Hebrew word that refers to the precepts commanded by God. Its secondary meaning is a "moral deed performed as a religious duty." A mitzvah hero, Avital later explained to me, is "someone who does good deeds out of their hearts and without any gain from it." Imagine the pride and honor I felt when Avital said she had chosen me to be her mitzvah hero.

Avital asked if she could interview me for her school project, and of course I said I'd love to. We set up a time to talk on the phone. The interview was amazing—Avital had spent the weekend working on her questions and was completely prepared, like a little cub reporter. At the end of our talk, I asked her more about the project and how she would be presenting our story.

Then I surprised myself by asking, "Avital, would you like for me to come to your school when you present your project?"

There was silence on the phone. "My mom told me not to ask you to come," she finally said. "She said it would be stepping over the line." Then I heard her yell, "Mom! Ms. Schroff just asked if she could come to my school!" There was so much excitement in her voice, but the truth was, I was every bit as excited as she was, and probably more.

The day of the project, I drove to Avital's school and walked into a large room filled with students and their families. Suddenly, this adorable young girl with light brown hair and a contagious smile ran up to me and handed me flowers. Then she hugged me, and I hugged her back. I hadn't expected the moment to be so emotional, but it was. Something about this young girl appreciating my story, and being inspired by it, filled me with hope and joy.

I sat and listened to Avital read her essay aloud. "In my interview with Ms. Schroff, I asked her what she wanted *me* to learn from her acts of kindness," Avital read. "She said she wanted me to learn how one small act of kindness can make a big difference."

Avital also spoke about *tikkun olam*, a Jewish value that means "repairing the world." "We are taught that we should take action and make the world a better place," she explained. "I feel that Ms. Schroff's acts were miraculous and showed *tikkun olam*. In the Talmud, there is a saying: 'Whoever saves a life, it is considered as if he saves an entire world.' Laura's actions repaired Maurice's world."

Then Avital gave her presentation, and it was beautiful. She had mounted text and photos detailing the story of Maurice and me on big black boards, condensing our long history—Maurice and I met thirty years ago—into a dramatic representation of the profound consequences of a single loving act. Avital had even crafted a miniature table with two place settings and a batch of pint-size chocolate chip cookies—a representation of all the times Maurice and I had baked and shared cookies.

An Invisible Thread has won a couple of awards and been praised by lots of different people. But even so, I can't think of any honor that means more to me than Avital naming me her mitzvah hero.

That day, Avital ran over and handed me something else. It was a tiny slip of paper—the fortune from a fortune cookie she'd cracked open the weekend before. It read, "Give what you have to someone, it may be better than you dare think."

To this day, that tiny slip of paper sits on my desk, reminding me of my sweet little friend, Avital.

And yet, the true wonder of Avital's story is not her school project or our meeting, but rather what happened one month *after* I met her at her school.

It was Avital's mother, Rachel, who first brought my story to her attention. "She was reading the book, and then she gave it to me and we started reading it together," says Avital. Before learning about Maurice and his difficult childhood in a series of welfare hotels, "I didn't really know how harsh someone's life could be," she says. "Reading about Maurice was like culture shock, and it really made me grateful for all the things I have."

One month after we met, Avital and her mother drove to a local supermarket to buy groceries for dinner. After finishing their shopping, they got in the car and began leaving the parking lot. "As we were driving, we saw a man holding up a sign," Avital says. "In the sign, he said he needed help. He asked for food and milk and diapers."

They drove past the man on their way out of the lot. All of a sudden, Avital spoke up. "Mom," she said, "we have to go back."

Her mother looked startled. "I actually said to her, 'Avital, it's dinnertime; we have to get home,'" Rachel remembers. "And she just said, very forcefully, 'No, Mom, we have to go back. We have to *do something*.'"

Was that the first time Avital had ever driven past someone asking for help? Probably not. But it *was* the first time she ever really noticed.

"I had just spoken with you a month before," Avital explained to me. "And what you did for Maurice really meant something to me. And then I had the chance to do something like that in my own life, too."

Rachel turned the car around and went back. They went into Walmart and bought diapers, wet wipes, milk, bread, even some Hostess donuts. Then they came out and looked for the man with the sign. When they found him, Avital handed him the bags filled with supplies. "He was surprised," says Rachel. "And then all of a sudden his wife came out of the shadows with their two small children. She came out to thank us, too."

For Avital, the moment was one she will never, ever forget. "I remember how good it made me feel," she says. "I felt like this family could make it through one more day. We went back many times after that to find them, but we never saw them again."

Even so, something had changed in Avital. Something had been activated.

"Ever since then, she has not stopped doing things like that," says her mother. "Every time we stop at a light and see someone asking for money, she says, 'Mom, we have to give them something. We have to do something.'"

"What we give them won't make a difference to us," Avital says, "but it might make a really big difference for them."

~~~≈≶⊃~~~

Avital's good deed in the parking lot of a Walmart, and her continuing efforts to help those in need, make her *my* mitzvah hero.

In a way, Avital allowed me to discover how children as young as eleven—and even younger—can recognize and honor their own invisible threads and become angels on earth.

Avital's act of kindness in the parking lot, then, was more than just one simple loving gesture. It was a Life Lesson—both for her and for me. It changed the way both of us see and think about the world.

"Ever since we bought those groceries, I do look around a lot more for opportunities to help, pretty much everywhere I go," Avital says. "I pay a lot more attention to everyone—kids, teenagers, adults. I'm looking around for who needs help."

Now the challenge for Avital will be to hold on to as much of that beautiful purity of heart as she can.

"I don't know exactly what I want to do when I grow up," Avital told me. "But I do know that part of my life will always be helping others. I will always look for the chance to show someone I care about them."

PART THREE
OUTWARDNESS

Can't we live perfectly fine lives without thinking about invisible threads? Without worrying about being angels on earth? I suppose we can. But I don't think we should. The glory of existence, the real payoff to being alive, happens in the company of others. The stories in this section taught me that living life in an outward way is vital to our happiness and well-being. To live outwardly is to understand that we are not only connected to one another but responsible for one another, too.

9

THE DONOR

Jason Bradburn is thirty-four and a senior vice president at Morgan Stanley. He followed his older brother, Mark, into the world of finance and found he loved the work. A few years ago, he heard that someone prominent in the financial community—someone he had met and casually knew—had been diagnosed with an extremely rare blood disorder. "His name was Alan, and he had young twin daughters," Jason says. "He was highly established in the finance industry, but all the money in the world couldn't fix his problem."

The only potential solution, Jason learned, was a peripheral blood stem cell or bone marrow transplant. Both Jason and Mark agreed to enter the National Marrow Donor Program through an organization called Be The Match, in hope of helping Alan.

"I walked five minutes to Alan's office and someone there swabbed the inside of my cheek for thirty seconds," Jason recalls. "It was easier than giving blood. I walked out of there thinking, 'Well, this is a nice thing we're doing.' But really, it couldn't have been easier."

Neither Jason nor his brother was a match. Sadly, no match was found for Alan, and he passed away.

Over time, being part of the database became an afterthought for Jason. Occasionally, he'd get a notice from Be The Match confirming his commitment to the program and updating his contact information. "I didn't give it much thought at all," he says. "I'd send the notice back and tell them I was still in, and that was that."

Nearly three years passed.

Then one day Jason was on his way to Michigan to see a client. He was going through airport security when his cell phone went off. It was someone from Be The Match.

"I thought it was a solicitation," Jason says. "I told them I'd call them back."

It wasn't a solicitation.

A caseworker explained to Jason that he'd come up as a potential match for a patient who might need a transplant. Would he go to a blood center and have five vials of blood drawn to confirm he was a match?

Jason said he would. A few weeks after being tested at a New York City blood center, Jason got a letter in the mail from Be The Match. "I thought that because it was a letter, that meant I wasn't a match," he says. "Then I read it: 'We have done the testing and you are a match for a patient who potentially needs a donation. We will contact you if and when we are ready to proceed.'"

To Jason, it still seemed a long way from actually becoming a donor. "The letter was formal and didn't tell me anything about the patient," he says. "It was impersonal. My impression was that they want to keep it that way, until it becomes personal."

A month later, the second call came. "They told me that they still weren't sure they were going to need me, but they arranged for me to get a full physical exam just in case," Jason says. "It would be the most thorough physical of my life—heart, kidney, liver, everything. They told me it was for my safety, not the patient's."

Jason came out with a clean bill of health. It still didn't seem as if he were actually being asked to *do* anything to help someone. It didn't feel real. "For one thing, they hardly tell you anything at all about the patient," he says. "All I knew was that he was a male, sixty years old, and living somewhere in the United States. And that he had myelodysplastic syndrome, or MDS, which hinders the production of blood cells. But that was it. That was all I knew."

Just a week after his physical exam, the third call came.

"We need you," the caseworker said. "We are ready to go."

The procedure would involve spinning every drop of Jason's blood in and out of his body one and a half times in order to extract a donation of peripheral blood stem cells, which are located within his white blood cells. He would also have to take a chemotherapy-type drug that had not been approved by the FDA for healthy patients. The drug would give him severe flu-like symptoms and joint pain— so bad, he was told, it might be hard to walk. It wasn't anywhere near what some patients go through, he realized, but neither was it a routine, pain-free procedure. Jason's mother, for one, worried about the long-term effects the donation might have on Jason's health.

Still, the decision to move forward belonged entirely to Jason. There was no contract, no binding obligation. He could back out at any time, including right before the actual donation. For that reason, his caseworker spent a lot of time on the phone with Jason, explaining the nature of the commitment he'd be making.

"She said I could be the patient's only chance for survival in the world," Jason remembers. "It was pretty heavy stuff. What's more, the patient needs to get massive amounts of chemotherapy before the donation—enough to kill him. So if I show up on the day of the donation and change my mind, the patient most likely would die."

The caseworker kept asking Jason, "Do you understand the commitment? Are you still willing to proceed?" There was no middle ground—either Jason was in or out.

"It's one thing if your brother calls you and says he needs a kidney," Jason says. "I would give my life for my brother. But a stranger? A complete stranger? We don't often think about other people's illnesses that way. Usually we just say, 'Oh, that's too bad for them,' and we get on with our lives."

Jason still had that option. He could still say, "That's too bad," and get on with his life. But all along he knew that wasn't really ever an option.

"I remember telling my mother, 'If this was someone in our family who was sick, we would want someone to step up and make the donation,'" he says. "It was that simple. If you can give hope to someone when you have it to give, then you *have* to give it. Someone needed me. How could I not help?"

Jason took the unapproved drug—six straight days of two injections every morning—and came down with all the symptoms he'd been warned about: the worst flu-like symptoms he'd ever felt and increasing pain in his bones and joints. Five days before the procedure, he was told to avoid any risky behavior. "As a New Yorker, I used to jaywalk all the time. I remember stopping even that," says Jason. "I realized I had this antidote in my body, and I had to be mindful of that. That's when it all became real. I was no longer responsible for just my life. I was responsible for someone else's life, too."

He went to Manhattan's Memorial Sloan Kettering Hospital for the actual donation. He sat in a bed with an IV going into one arm and coming out the other. At any given time, one pint of his blood would be out of his body until all the blood in his body was funneled through a centrifuge that stripped out the white blood cells. The procedure took three hours, and he was told it would be exhausting—like the feeling of running a marathon. "Your heart has to pump intensely for three hours," he says. "But again, it was all manageable. It was nothing like what the patient probably had to go through."

In the middle of the procedure, a doctor came in and thanked Jason for his sacrifice. "This is why I practice medicine," the doctor told him. "We could have the best techniques, the best technology in the world, but if we didn't have the human element—if we didn't have *your blood*—we couldn't do what we need to do."

Then the procedure was over, and a small IV bag had been filled with Jason's white blood cells. The bag was put into a cooler and whisked out of the room. Mark had been with him throughout the procedure, and he helped him leave the hospital and walk to the sidewalk to get a cab. But it was pouring rain, and there weren't any cabs in sight. "Finally a taxi came out of nowhere and picked us up," Jason says. "Mark dropped me off at my apartment and kept going to his office."

Only later did Jason learn the elderly cabbie was another one of the world's kind souls. "He told Mark that when it's raining hard, he always drives to hospitals, because he doesn't want sick people to have to stand in the rain," Jason says. The cabbie had also heard Jason and Mark talking about the procedure, and at the end of the ride he turned around and spoke to Mark.

"He told him, 'That was the most incredible story I've ever heard, and it was an honor for me to drive you two,'" Jason says. "Then he refused to charge Mark for the ride." The memory makes Jason well up with tears. "I mean, I work in *finance*," he says. "And here is this cabbie, and he doesn't know me, and he will never see me again, and he needs the money much more than I do, and still he didn't want to charge us. When my brother told me that, we were both in tears. There is so much bad that happens in the world. And then you meet someone like this cabbie."

Jason knew it would be a while before he would hear anything about the patient. In fact, two full months passed without an update. He didn't know if the donation had helped, or even if the patient was still alive.

He was driving from New York City to Rochester with his girl-friend, Liza—now his wife—when he got the call. It was his case-worker, and she had an update.

"It was positive," Jason says. "Normally, they keep recipients in the hospital for thirty days. They let this patient go home in seventeen days. It was a very big, very positive step."

About six months later, Jason got another update. This time, there had been a setback, and the patient had to go back to the hospital. Today, Jason is awaiting more updates, which don't come as often as he'd like. "I realize he might not survive, and that has made me think about what it is that I gave this man," he says. "And I realize that what I gave him is time. The gift of time. More time with his family, more time to live. That has made me appreciate, probably for the first time, the true value of time."

The terms of Jason's donation stated that for twelve months, his personal information would be withheld from the patient. But after a year it would be released, and the patient could decide if he wanted to meet the donor or not. A few years have passed since Jason's donation, and he hasn't heard anything from the patient yet. "I don't know if I'll ever get the chance to meet him," he says. "I would like to, but I don't know." It is possible, then, that the recipient of Jason's white blood cells might forever remain a perfect stranger.

Except that is not entirely true.

"This man has changed my entire outlook on humanity," Jason says. "He has made me realize we are all connected; we are all bound to other people. I used to walk down the street and not really notice people, but now I look at everyone and think, 'That could be the guy. That could be him.' I am really seeing people for the first time."

There is something else that has changed Jason's perspective of the world. Once his white blood cells were given to the patient, the patient's body would begin to produce new white blood cells. But even those cells *would still be Jason's cells.*

"Think about that," he says. "He has my blood cells in his body. We tricked his body into thinking that my healthy cells are his. But they will always be *my cells.*"

In fact, white blood cell donations have been known to change the patient's appearance and make the recipient look more like the donor.

"I mean, this guy could end up taking on some of my traits, which is surreal," Jason says. "I've never had any kind of relationship like that."

His may be an exceptional case—an example of how an act of kindness can draw us ever closer together—but to Jason, the lesson of his experience is universal.

"What it shows is how strongly we are *all* connected in this world," he says. "We are all part of one great big community, and we are all responsible for one another."

LUCKY US

I can't think of a better way to describe being an angel on earth than by using Jason's words—we become angels when we realize that we are responsible for one another.

If we begin to think this way, something remarkable happens. We begin to turn outward. We see the world differently. We are changed in a very real way. For Jason, this shift in perspective allowed him to, as he put it, really see people for the first time. That doesn't sound like a small fringe benefit to me. In fact, it sounds monumental! Life-changing!

This, too, is what outwardness means—an understanding that we are not only responsible for one another, but that we are blessed to be so!

"All I did was get lucky," says Jason, reflecting on his act of kindness. "I was just luckier than anyone else in the registry, because I was the one who got the chance to help."

Lucky us—we get chances to be angels on earth all the time.

10

THE TWENTY-FIVE TACOS

Jose Luis Balleza cannot remember her name.

It was a long time ago—nearly four decades—and he was only six years old at the time. He has tried to remember it, tried to summon it from somewhere deep in his brain, but it's no use. She doesn't have a name anymore. It has been lost to time.

But the woman herself, and what she did—this, he will never forget.

"I think about her all the time," says Jose. "I remember her all the time. She taught me a lesson that really changed my life."

Jose was a young boy living in the Mexican town of Reynosa—the border town to Hidalgo, Texas—with his mother and father and five siblings. His father drove taxis and trucks for a living, but when he fell ill at an early age, he could no longer work. "All I remember was that he would be lying in his sickbed all day," says Jose. "And then one day the bed was not there, and my father was not there. He was just gone."

Jose was six when his father's death plunged the family further into poverty. "There was no safety net," he says. "No pension, no welfare, no savings, nothing. There were no relatives to help us, and my mother had to stay home to take care of us. We had to survive somehow on our own."

Jose's mother, Maria Ana, came up with a plan. She would

cook tacos at home and send her eldest sons, Jose and Martin, who was nine, into the streets to sell them. "Every morning she would cook them with eggs and beans, and she would wrap them in a little bit of foil, and she would give Martin fifty of them to sell, and because I was younger she gave me twenty-five," remembers Jose. "I carried them all in a big steel pot to keep them warm. And I took a bottle of salsa with me."

Jose's job was to sell all twenty-five tacos for a peso each—or roughly eight cents—before 1:00 p.m., when he had to go to the afternoon session of school. "My mother was very clear with us," he says. "She said, 'Okay, you are going to sell *all* these tacos.' We didn't have a choice. We had to find a way to sell all the tacos."

At first, Maria Ana sent him out with his older sister, who was eight. But Jose felt she only slowed him down. He told his mother he was fine by himself, and she agreed to let him go out alone.

Jose hauled his steel pot into downtown Reynosa, near the railroad tracks and the cantinas and the bus station. It was the most dangerous part of town, but that's where the people were, so that's where he had to be. He was frightened and timid at first, but fairly quickly became a good salesman. He even developed a sales pitch.

"Someone would walk by and I'd say, 'With salsa or no salsa?'" he recalls. "And they'd say, 'Salsa for what?' And I'd say, 'These delicious tacos.' It worked a lot."

One morning, a teenager asked Jose for two tacos. Jose was suspicious, because not many people ever bought two tacos. Still, he handed them to the teen, who said he only had a twenty-peso bill and needed change. Jose kept his pesos tightly bundled deep in his pocket, and he knew never to take them out in front of anyone. But the teen insisted. Jose took out his pesos, and the teen grabbed them and ran.

"I tried to chase after him with my steel pot, but I couldn't catch him," Jose says. "I was afraid to go back home that day with no money."

Another morning, Jose ducked into a run-down pool hall to sell tacos. One man bought a taco, and then tried to lure Jose into the bathroom. "He pressured me with money," Jose says. "I was only six years old. Fortunately, someone else came by and stopped it. I was extremely careful after that."

No matter how careful he was, Jose was constantly in danger. He was a child in the worst part of town, vulnerable to all kinds of harm. Still, he peddled his tacos everywhere—in cantinas with signs that read NO CHILDREN, in seedy stores by the railroad tracks, in bars filled with drunks and hustlers. He had no choice—he had to sell his twenty-five tacos. Sometimes, if he was very lucky, he sold them all in just a couple of hours. Most of the time, he had to stay on the dangerous streets for several hours, walking an average of three miles a day, lugging his big steel pot.

Then came the morning when Jose slipped into the bus station and noticed a young woman in an office. She was a secretary, or perhaps a ticket taker. Jose went into her office and asked if she wanted a taco.

The woman stopped what she was doing and looked at the boy.

"You haven't been selling tacos very long," she said. "I know all the other boys selling newspapers and tacos, and I haven't seen you."

"Only two months," Jose said.

"How old are you?"

"Six."

"Are you going to school?"

"Yes, ma'am."

"Okay, what is the name of your school?"

She wanted to see if Jose was lying. But he wasn't, and he told her he went to an elementary school called Venustiano Carranza. In his mind, Jose thought, "Is she going to buy a taco or not?"

"You are too young to be out on the street selling tacos," the woman said, "especially in this area."

"I have no choice," Jose told her. "My father passed away."

The woman paused and looked sympathetically at Jose.

"I am sorry about your father," she said. "I will buy three tacos."

Three tacos! No one bought three tacos. Two at most, but usually just one. "Maybe she's really hungry," Jose thought. "Maybe she will save them to eat later." Either way, it was an excellent sale.

Jose pocketed his three pesos and started to run off, but the woman stopped him.

"What is your name?" she asked.

"Jose."

"Jose, listen to me," she said. "I want you to come see me every day. And no matter how many tacos you have left, I will buy them from you."

Jose could hardly believe it. The next day, he returned to the bus station to see the woman. But he didn't bring all twenty-five tacos—he knew that was not what she'd meant. He didn't feel it would be right to ask her to buy so many. So he hustled as he always did and showed up in her office with five tacos.

The woman bought them all.

Jose went to see the woman every day for three months. By buying so many tacos from him, she cut at least an hour and usually much more off his normal shift, taking him off the dangerous streets, making him less vulnerable.

"I probably sold five thousand tacos in my life," says Jose, "and she was the only person who ever said, 'Come to me and I will buy your tacos.' She even once bought a bag of groceries for me to bring back home."

Fairly quickly, Jose realized the woman's motives had nothing to do with her appetite. "Everyone else bought tacos because they were hungry," he says. "She bought them because she didn't want me on the streets and exposed to danger."

Eventually, Jose's mother decided to go to the United States to try to make a living there. She took two of his brothers and left Jose behind with his older brother and sister. Without Maria Ana to cook the tacos, Jose could no longer sell them. Instead, he made money by helping people carry shopping bags across the international bridge between the United States and Mexico.

Some days, he thought about the woman who'd bought so many tacos from him. But he never had time to go back and see her.

In fact, he never saw her again.

In time, Jose joined his mother in Texas. He began his education and graduated in the top two percent of his high school class. There was no money for him to go to college, so he began working, first as a clerk in a supply store, but soon in positions that normally required a college degree. Eventually, he earned a bachelor's degree, and he also became the youngest congregation elder in his church. His tireless work ethic, Jose says, came from his mother, Maria Ana. "She is seventy-four, and she has worked nearly six decades of her life to take care of her children," he says.

Jose has a family of his own now: he has been married to Oralia for twenty-six years, and together they have a daughter, Krystal, and a son, Luis Alberto. Jose regularly volunteers as a spiritual advisor at a south Texas state prison, and sometimes he conducts a prison witnessing program for inmates. He also works as a mentor for youngsters and young couples, helping them cope with personal and psychological problems, as well as challenges like transportation and acceptance into schools.

"Sometimes I will mentor a couple who has a child around six years old, and I will think back to myself at that age," he says. "The reason I am a mentor now is because it is a way for me to repay the kindness that this woman paid to me so many years ago."

Over the years, Jose has shared the story of the woman with different people, and not all of them have had the same reaction. "Some might say, 'Oh, well, she didn't give you a scholarship or give you money,'" he says. "'She didn't even buy all of your tacos.' But the thing is, she didn't *need* to. At that moment, all I needed was for someone to show me they cared, someone to be a good customer. And that was more than enough for me. I didn't need anything else."

All these years later, Jose can only hope that the woman who bought his tacos understands the impact of what she did. He has no way to find her, but if he did, he would love to tell her that her simple act of kindness remains embedded in his heart. Because what Jose now realizes—what has changed the way he looks at the world—is that the woman did so much more for him than simply buy his tacos.

"It was not about the money," Jose says. "It was that she said, 'Keep coming back.' It was that she *cared* about me. That is why I will remember her forever. She made my life better, and she taught me a valuable lesson: if it is in your hands to help someone, then do it, because you cannot realize how important that one little gesture may be."

INSPIRATION

One of the best Christmas presents I ever received didn't come from a store. It didn't cost anything, and it wasn't wrapped. It was the gift Maurice sneaked under my tree on the first Christmas we spent together, back in 1986.

It was a white teddy bear with a little red heart.

I knew the backstory of the bear. Up to the time I met him, Maurice had been given only two presents his entire life—a little toy Hess truck from one of his uncles, and, from Grandma Rose, a joint.

The Christmas before we met, Maurice went to the Salvation Army and got to pick a donated toy from a bin. The toy he chose was the white teddy bear. It was his one and only toy—literally, the only thing he had to give in the world. And he gave it to me.

Being an angel on earth is not always about sweeping gestures or enormous generosity. When we talk about being responsible for one another, it doesn't always mean we are literally responsible for someone's health and happiness and well-being over the course of a lifetime.

It means we may be responsible for those things in one particular moment of need.

Maurice's kind and simple gesture toward me changed the way I thought about Christmas—and about giving.

Over the last five years I've heard about hundreds of similar gestures, and hearing about them has changed me, too.

I understand now why even the smallest act of kindness and compassion can be unfathomably powerful. It's because a single small act can change the way we think. It can change the way we see the world, and it can motivate us to achieve things we never thought possible.

Kindness is inspirational. And one of the most powerful things angels on earth give us is inspiration.

Because with inspiration, we become capable of greatness.

_____

11

THE SIX CUPS OF COFFEE

Deland Hawk was born in Ponemah, a small town on the Red Lake Nation in Minnesota. He was a member of the Ojibwa—the fourth largest group of Native Americans after the Navajo, Cherokee, and Lakota. At eighteen, Deland joined the marine corps and served in Vietnam. When he came home, he started a family—his wife, Angie, and their two daughters, Pam and Sheila.

But then, in 1999, at the age of forty-seven, Deland died of a heart attack.

Then the Veterans Administration denied Angie's claim for a widow's pension.

After that, Angie and her daughters became homeless.

⁘

I learned about Angie and Deland through a man named Wendell Affield, who wrote to me after reading *An Invisible Thread*. He had a story to tell—an amazing story—but he didn't want to tell it. He is not one to talk a lot about himself or draw attention to things he's done. It was Angie Hawk who pushed Wendell to write and tell me their story.

"People need to know," she said.

Wendell grew up about fifteen miles away from the Red Lake

Nation, on a small farm in a former logging town called Nebish. He spent his life farming and managing a butcher shop, and he still lives in Minnesota with Patti, his wife of forty years.

Like Deland Hawk, Wendell served in the U.S. military and did a tour in Vietnam. And like Deland, he came home haunted by the ghosts of war. He first met Deland in 1992, at a meeting for veterans struggling with post-traumatic stress disorder, or PTSD. "Deland was a good man with a good family," Wendell says. "He had strong beliefs that came from the traditions of the Ojibwa."

At the time of his death, Deland was receiving a Veterans Administration pension for post-traumatic stress disorder, as well as ischemic heart disease, which is linked to exposure to Agent Orange, a highly toxic herbicide used as a weapon by U.S. forces during the Vietnam War. An autopsy of his body would have revealed that ischemic heart disease caused his heart attack, making his death war-related—and making his widow, Angie, eligible for benefits.

But there was no autopsy.

When Deland died, he had a traditional Ojibwa burial, as was his wish. But Ojibwa custom prohibits autopsies, and without the verification of his heart disease that an autopsy would have provided, the coroner who examined Deland's body was forced to list the reason for his passing as simply "natural causes."

Because of that, the Veterans Administration denied Angie's claim.

"That made me really angry," Wendell says. "Deland was good enough to serve his country in Vietnam, but not good enough to be treated fairly by the government."

Wendell points out that the military and the Veterans Administration honor and respect many religious beliefs—just not, it seemed to him, Native American beliefs. "It was frustrating," he says. After the claim was denied, Wendell lost track of Angie and her daughters. "I assumed they'd gone on their way somewhere. But then six months after Deland died, Angie and her family showed up on our farm, homeless and hungry."

Without continuing benefits from the VA, Angie could no longer afford to pay rent. Wendell and Patti helped them find housing, but still, Angie's struggles continued. She stayed with friends until she wore out her welcome. She stayed at homeless shelters until the clock ran out. She found subsidized housing, but the rent and utility bills always piled up, leading to evictions. "We watched her go from place to place and apartment to apartment," Wendell says, "and along the way her family got broken up."

One of Angie's daughters got in trouble with the law and lost her children to foster care. Then the same thing happened to her other daughter.

"I was watching her family fall apart," Wendell says. "I felt so powerless; I didn't think there was anything I could do. I also had this awful feeling of guilt. Guilt that I was alive, and Deland was dead."

Wendell stayed in touch with Angie and often brought her boxes of food wherever she was staying. One winter, Angie was living in a small apartment in a crumbling building across the street from a homeless shelter. Wendell boxed up some deer meat, got in his truck, and went to see his friend.

He knocked on the front door, and Angie let him in. What he saw shocked him.

"It was this horrible, blighted place," he says. "There was barely any insulation, and the snow on the roof was melting, and water was pouring down from the ceiling and ripping away the ceiling tiles."

But it wasn't the squalor that truly surprised Wendell.

It was the six men sitting at Angie's small kitchen table.

Wendell looked them over and tried to figure out who they were and what they were doing there. They were Native American, and they were huddled in winter coats. He put the box of deer meat on the counter and whispered to Angie, "Who are these guys?"

"They are from the homeless shelter," Angie said. "The shelter locks them out during the day, and they have nowhere to go."

Wendell looked at the six men again. They were sipping from steaming mugs of coffee that Angie had made for them. Inches away, a stream of water poured down from the ceiling into a bucket, while the winter cold blasted through the front door. The six men nodded at Wendell and went back to sipping their coffee.

And in that moment, something inside Wendell was changed.

"I was inspired," he says. "Here was this woman at the bottom of her journey, and she still had compassion for these six homeless men. She had literally almost nothing—the clothes on her back, a little bit of food. And yet she still shared what she had with other people in need. I was amazed by her. I was taken aback by her big, sharing heart."

In fact, sharing with others is a bedrock principle of the Ojibwa. "In our culture, it's usually, 'What's mine is mine,'" Wendell says. "But not to Angie. For her, it's all about sharing. It is about extended family. It is about helping one another."

———≈———

The six cups of coffee spurred Wendell into action. That night, he went home and started reading through Angie's VA claims again.

On the face of it, it was a lost cause. With Wendell's help, Angie had appealed the case all the way to the Board of Veterans'

Appeals—the highest rung of the ladder. But with no new information, a reversal of the VA's decision seemed impossible. "The claim was going nowhere," Wendell says. "Without an autopsy, the VA would not change its decision. But I went through all the documents again anyway. I kept thinking, 'There has to be something here, some detail that can get this going again.'"

Then Wendell narrowed his focus to Deland's death certificate—the one that listed the reason for his passing as "natural causes." He'd looked at it dozens of times, but he looked at it with fresh eyes, and he saw something he hadn't realized before.

"I noticed the coroner's name, and all of a sudden I said, 'I know him!'" Wendell recalls. "His wife and my wife had done Bible study group together."

Wendell called up the coroner, Mark, and explained Angie's situation.

"Is there any way you can go back and look at her case again?" he asked.

Mark said he would.

Just a few days later, Mark sent Wendell an email with a newly written statement he was appending to Deland's death certificate.

"I would like to emphasize that when I do not have autopsy proof of cause of death, I always sign the death certificate as 'natural causes' unless other evidence indicates the death was accidental, homicidal, or suicidal," Mark wrote in the statement. "Consequently, the death certificate notation of 'natural causes' does not mean that the patient did not have a cardiac condition."

"On the contrary," Mark's statement went on, "the history in this case suggests to me that most likely *this man did in fact die of a cardiac condition, namely ischemic heart disease.*"

Wendell hand-delivered the statement to his local Veterans Services Office. An officer there faxed the statement to the VA regional office in Fargo, North Dakota, and requested that the appeal be expedited because of Angie's dire situation.

Three weeks later, Wendell got a call from a VSO officer. The officer told him, "The claim has been approved."

Wendell choked up on the phone. "I knew right then that Angie's problems would be alleviated," he says. "She would start getting benefits, and she could get a stable home, and maybe she could put her family back together."

Yet Wendell wasn't at all prepared for what he heard next.

The Veterans Administration hadn't merely approved the reinstatement of Angie's benefits. They had also made that approval *retroactive*. Which meant Angie wouldn't just start receiving new benefits. She would also receive a lump sum representing all the benefits she'd lost during the years her claim had been denied.

"I was shocked," Wendell says. "I was amazed. I knew how important this was for Angie. We could get her into a safe neighborhood now."

The VSO officer asked Wendell if he could contact Angie to tell her the news. Wendell was happy to, except for one thing.

He didn't know how to reach her.

She was no longer in the subsidized apartment. She wasn't in any shelter. She had no phone, and no one knew where she was.

Angie Hawk was missing.

———⁂———

Wendell's only hope was that somehow Angie would reach out to him. "That had happened before," he says. "When she was truly down-and-out, she would get ahold of me. But sometimes weeks would go by without any word. I just didn't know."

As fate would have it, the contact came that very afternoon, when Wendell got a phone call from Angie's daughter Pam.

"My mother is sitting in a ditch, and she is too tired to go on," Pam told Wendell. "Can you help?"

Angie had been evicted yet again, and she and her daughter were hitchhiking to another homeless shelter. But no one would pick them up, and after walking for hours Angie was too exhausted to take another step. So she sat in a ditch on the edge of town, raising her bare hands to try to block the hot sun.

That would be the last day Angie would have nowhere to go.

When Wendell finally told Angie and her daughter the news about the claim, "they were just ecstatic," he says. "We were all ecstatic. Lots of giant hugs. Angie knew her life had just changed."

"I still think about the irony of that moment," Wendell says. "There was this big pile of money on one side of the scale, and on the other was this woman who was literally at the end of her path."

Today, five years later, Angie owns a modest but comfortable house in Minnesota. The retroactive benefits she received allowed her to buy it outright, with no mortgage, and she moved both her daughters in with her. Some of her grandchildren are home from foster care, and Angie continues to work on reintegrating the rest of them. Angie also makes room for friends who are homeless or struggling. Except now, she can offer them a bit more than just coffee.

"She lives in town, so I stop by and see them quite often," says Wendell, who helped Angie pick out the right house and get the best deal. "There are all these people and kids running around. It is a busy, bustling home."

At the center of it all is Angie.

"She is a very gracious person," Wendell says. "She is always so thankful and so grateful for her home. Even now, sometimes people will come by and want to take her with them somewhere, and she'll say, 'No, I want to stay right here. I want to stay in my house.'"

Wendell still brings Angie boxes of meat; that has become their little ritual. Recently, Wendell took Angie to the office of a local attorney and helped her draw up a trust for her grandchildren. When Angie signed the final paperwork, she looked up at Wendell with a big smile.

"Never will my grandchildren be homeless," she said proudly.

Wendell had no intention of sharing the story of how he helped Angie with anyone, and he almost certainly wouldn't have, had Angie not asked him one last favor.

"You must tell people what you did," she pleaded. "It might save another widow from going through what I went through."

So Wendell went home and sat at his desk and wrote an email to me.

"Helping others creates a bond that is difficult for some people to understand," Wendell began his letter. "Fifteen years ago, a family came to me for help . . ."

TAKE FEWER SELFIES

Over the last five years I've become more aware of the power of outward thinking, and that has changed the way I live.

I believe I have always been a thoughtful, considerate person, but because I have been exposed to so many angels on earth, I now try to frame every decision I make in terms of my interconnectedness to other people.

In any given interaction with someone, I'll ask, "How can I make things better not only for me, but also for them? What can I do to improve not only my situation, but theirs, too? Is there a way I can make a positive difference for both of us here?"

Again, I'm not talking about making major sacrifices or neglecting my own needs. I'm talking about small adjustments. For instance, whenever I'm asked to give a speech, I spend a lot of time figuring out how I can deliver the best possible experience for the people who have invited me. What can I do to make it an easier arrangement for them? Can I show up earlier? Stay later? Tailor my speech to their specific needs?

These questions may lead to only a small difference in the actual outcome. But what I've found is that, by asking them, I've made the exchange more fulfilling for everyone involved, not least of all myself.

And all I had to do was focus a little less on myself and a little more on the world around me.

I guess it's like the difference between taking a selfie and taking a regular photo.

A selfie greatly narrows our field of vision.

But turning the camera outward opens the whole world to us.

12

THE SWEATER

Eileen Pacheco Schwartz was seventeen, and she wanted a new sweater.

She was one of six sisters, and she wore her share of hand-me-downs, and she wanted something new. A customer had left a copy of *Woman's Day* on a table at the pizza parlor where Eileen worked as a waitress in Portland, Oregon, so she sat down for a few minutes to look through it for a sweater.

Eileen couldn't afford anything too expensive—she was working part-time and only making $4.20 an hour, and a lot of that had to go toward her high school tuition. "That was my father's rule," she says. "I loved music, and my parents agreed to send me to a private Catholic school with a really good music program. But my father said I had to get straight A's, and I had to get a job and contribute toward the tuition."

That didn't leave much extra money for Eileen, but somehow she stretched out her paychecks and still had enough to buy a new sweater. So she leafed through the magazine, hoping to find one she liked.

Instead, she found a photo of a boy.

"It was one of those ads for the Christian Children's Fund," Eileen says. "It said where the boy was from, and how his family were farmers, and how they needed our help." The ad featured a pledge card and asked readers to send it in and donate fifteen dollars a month to needy children half a world away.

As Eileen read through the ad and looked at the little boy's sweet face, one thought and one thought only ran through her mind: "I thought, 'I don't really need that sweater.'"

⁂

That, after all, was how she'd been raised—to look for opportunities to help. "Both of my parents and particularly my father believed we were put on this earth to serve," she says. "He wanted us to wake up every morning and ask, 'Lord, how do you want me to serve you today?'"

Eileen mailed in the card and got back a letter about a boy in Guatemala. His name was Hipolito. "He was nine years old, and he was this little pudgy thing," she says. "In the photo he was standing in a cornfield, and he looked like he did not want to have his picture taken."

Eileen sent in her first check for fifteen dollars and, as requested, included a letter that the Children's Fund forwarded to Hipolito. The rules were strict: no identifying personal details. Eileen told the boy about where she lived, what her high school was like, how she was one of six sisters. "I also told him that I looked forward to being a part of his life," she says.

She had no idea if the letter would actually reach Hipolito—three thousand miles away in Guatemala—or, if it did, if he would ever write back. She stuck the boy's photo on the refrigerator with a magnet so she could see it every day, and she moved on with her busy teenage life.

One month later, there was a red-white-and-blue airmail envelope with her name on it in the mailbox. Eileen excitedly sat down to read it.

The first words were *Mi madrina*. Eileen asked her mother what that meant.

"He's calling you his godmother," her mom replied.

"I can still clearly remember what it felt like to have him call me that," Eileen says. "It was the most amazing thing in the world."

In the letter, Hipolito told Eileen all about his life. How his parents were farmers. How his village didn't have a post office. How he liked to play soccer. "Sweet little kid things like that," Eileen says. "And he thanked me. He always, always thanked me."

Each month, Eileen sent in her fifteen dollars, as well as a letter to Hipolito. And each month, she got one back from her "godson" in Guatemala. "He would always tell me about his school and how he was doing," she says. "I would be sent his grades, and they were really good. He was very smart. I later learned his father didn't want him to go to school. He wanted him to join him in the fields. But his mother insisted and found a way to get the money to send him to school."

Eileen didn't know how much of her fifteen dollars went toward Hipolito's education. She figured most of it went toward overhead, and maybe just a little bit helped out with his tuition. But as long as he was going to school and getting good grades, she was happy. "And every now and then, on his birthday and on holidays, I'd send him an extra five dollars, which was all they let us send," she says. "He'd write back and tell me what he bought with the money. It might be a soccer ball, but it would also be something like a pen. No matter what else he got, he always bought something for school."

Eileen also got new photos of Hipolito every year, and she

could see how fast he was growing. Before long, he was in high school—just as Eileen had been when they were first connected. Then Hipolito turned eighteen, the age when he could no longer be part of the Christian Children's Fund program. The sponsorship was over.

After nine years, Eileen and Hipolito could no longer be pen pals.

"He didn't have my address, and I didn't have his," Eileen says. "It was sad, but that's just the way it was."

What Eileen didn't know was that Hipolito had a mission: to thank her face-to-face.

First, he'd written to the program's administrators, asking for Eileen's address. But they refused to provide it. Then Hipolito flipped through all the photos Eileen had sent him, searching for clues. One of the last photos she'd mailed him was taken at her wedding, and it showed her and her new husband and all her sisters and bridesmaids. Hipolito reread the letter that came with the photo and noticed Eileen had mentioned her husband's name: David Schwartz. She wasn't supposed to have done it, but somehow it got through. Now Hipolito had what he needed—a lead.

Hipolito's path out of the cornfields took him all the way to Washington, D.C. He'd been awarded a scholarship through Georgetown University, and when he got to the Capitol he went straight to the Library of Congress. He found a Portland phone book and looked for the name Eileen Schwartz.

And right there, in tiny type, was Eileen's phone number.

It was seven o'clock one morning when her telephone rang.

"Hello?" she answered groggily.

"This is Hipolito," she heard a voice say. "Your godson from Guatemala."

Eileen felt her stomach do a flip. "I just couldn't believe it was him," she says. "I remember thinking, 'Gee, that doesn't sound like a nine-year-old.' But of course he wasn't a boy anymore. He was twenty-one."

Eileen made plans for Hipolito to come to Portland, so they could finally meet. At the airport, she worried for a moment that she might not recognize him—but only for a moment. "When he came out, I saw his bright, beautiful smile, and we ran to each other and hugged," she says. "It was so emotional." Eileen's family had come with her to the airport, and one of her sisters handed Hipolito a T-shirt that read, SOMEONE IN OREGON LOVES ME. "He took his shirt off and put the T-shirt right on," Eileen says. "It was the sweetest thing."

Hipolito stayed with Eileen and her family for two weeks. During that time, Eileen threw him a birthday party—the first birthday party he'd ever had. "He received all these nice presents—tennis shoes, a watch, a new suitcase, clothes—but his favorite thing was all the birthday cards people gave him," Eileen says. "He just gathered them up and held them in his hands. And every night I'd go to his bedroom to get him for dinner, and he'd be on the bed with all the birthday cards spread out. He loved reading them. He loved all the good wishes."

What struck Eileen most about Hipolito was how happy and lively he was. "He didn't have much of anything, but he was always smiling," she says. "He didn't care that he was poor."

Toward the end of his stay, Hipolito was in the kitchen with Eileen and her son Taylor, who was three. Suddenly, he pointed at the young boy.

"By the time Taylor graduates," he declared, "I will be Dr. Hipolito."

Eileen was so proud of him at that moment. But she also wondered how it would be possible. He had so little money, so little of anything. How was he going to make it all the way to a PhD?

~~~

Hipolito went back to Guatemala to work for two years, servicing an MRI machine at a medical clinic. Later on, he got a scholarship to attend a university in Heidelberg, Germany. He stayed in touch with Eileen, and back in Portland she followed his progress as closely as she could. "He was constantly pushing and pushing," she says. "But it was a long road."

It was on the Fourth of July in 2011—the year after Taylor graduated college—that she got a brief email from Hipolito.

"My *madrina*," it read, "I am writing to tell you that I have today received my PhD from the University of Heidelberg's Institute of Computer Science."

He was, at long last, Dr. Hipolito.

The email had only one more simple sentence: "*Madrina*, I am dedicating my PhD to you."

~~~

It took Hipolito twenty-one years to earn his PhD, but he never gave up, and today his plan is to get a teaching position back in his native Guatemala. "I learned so much from him," Eileen says. "He taught me that it doesn't matter how long it takes to achieve your dreams, as long as you do it. I am so proud of him, I can hardly explain it. He has given me so much more than I ever gave him."

In fact, Eileen did eventually learn how much of an impact her fifteen dollars a month had on Hipolito and his education.

She learned that it hadn't been minimal at all.

Her monthly fifteen dollars accounted for seventy-five percent of Hipolito's tuition.

Three-fourths of his tuition.

"His mother worked as a seamstress to come up with the other twenty-five percent," Eileen says. "She and I did this together."

For fifteen dollars a month, and one less sweater in her wardrobe, Eileen got something she will treasure forever—an unbreakable connection. "Hipolito has been one of the great blessings of my life," she says. "His friendship means so much to me. *So* much. He still calls me his *madrina*. And I still call him my godson."

13

THE HELPER'S HIGH

The more I traveled the country speaking about kindness and invisible threads, the more I began to wonder, "Is everything I'm saying true?"

Certainly, I was seeing plenty of evidence of how acts of kindness can change people's lives in very clear and profound ways. But invisible threads? Angels on earth? Were these things real?

And then—as so often happened in my amazing journey—I met just the right person at just the right time.

In 2013, I was invited to share my story on NBC's *Today* with Kathie Lee and Hoda. I'd been on the program before to share our invisible thread story. During that interview, Kathie Lee Gifford was so touched by our story, she got very emotional. About a year later, they invited me back on the show to talk about kindness in general. For that segment, I would be appearing alongside a "kindness expert" named Dr. Dale Atkins.

That "kindness expert" wound up changing the way I see the world.

Dale is a licensed psychologist and author who has been helping people improve their mental and emotional health for the past thirty years. She gives lectures, holds workshops, and appears on TV to talk about, in her words, "how people can live enriched, meaningful, healthy lives even as they navigate life's challenges."

Dale is also a wonderful, giving, lively woman who became my instant friend. After the segment, we agreed that we had our own invisible thread connection.

Our segment lasted only a few minutes, so I made it a point to stay in touch with Dale. She invited me to speak at an event for Jumpstart, a wonderful preschool literacy organization she's been involved with since its inception more than twenty years ago. I was happy to do it for several reasons, including that it gave me the chance to spend more time with Dale.

Because what I really wanted was Dale's insight into how being kind can change our life's path—and possibly turn us into angels.

"Human beings are hardwired to connect with people," Dale said to me in her typically cheerful and inspiring way when we met recently to talk about kindness. "We have an instinct to help others. Empathy is part of our evolution. We are social beings. But over time we are also taught to be cautious. To avoid potentially dangerous situations. That is why all those people walked right past Maurice on that street corner all those years ago. We can become cut off from our compassion."

I reminded Dale that I, too, walked right past Maurice, before turning around and going back to see him.

"What you did is face the suffering," Dale said. "You allowed yourself to be touched by the suffering. And when you do that, it becomes impossible to say, 'Oh, those poor people' and walk past them. When you look in someone's eyes and you feel what they're going through, that's when you are compelled to act."

Then I told Dale about all the classrooms I'd been in, and how children were probably my most receptive audience.

"Kids *love* kindness," she said. "They love it because they can feel it viscerally, with no layers. Sometimes we adults have to go through layers and layers of thoughts and defenses before we get to the real emotion. But kids don't have that. They instinctively respond to things that are a natural affirmation of the joy in life. It goes to a place that stimulates their brain in a positive way. They say, 'Wow, look how great it is that I can help someone else!'"

"To kids," Dale said, "kindness is like breathing—it's natural."

Dale was quick to credit all the researchers, scientists, and psychologists who came before her and who began to build this new way of looking at kindness and empathy. For instance, she explained, the term she used on *Today* with Kathie Lee and Hoda—"helper's high"—had been coined by Allan Luks, a researcher and author who's spent the last twenty years exploring, according to his website, the "powerful physical feelings people experience when directly helping others." As Dale puts it, "A helper's high is a feeling of moral elevation, of uplifting, and ultimately of well-being. Put simply, it means that when we help others, we help ourselves."

As an example, Dale cited a study of seriously ill patients who were deeply depressed. "The sicker they got, the more isolated and despondent they felt," Dale said. "But then they were encouraged to make phone calls to people who had been newly diagnosed with debilitating diseases. And the results were unbelievable! Their depression scores went down, they reported being in less pain, they expressed a desire to interact with others—their own health dramatically improved, and all because of a fifteen-minute phone call!"

In fact, Dale told me, just the action of watching someone do something kind—not doing it yourself, just *watching* someone do it—can give you the benefits of the helper's high. "There is a study in which some people viewed a video of funny, silly things, while other people viewed a video of Mother Teresa tending to the poor in Calcutta," Dale said. "The people who watched Mother Teresa underwent major physiological changes. They experienced positive feelings. And they maintained those positive feelings for one solid hour afterward. Across the board, they were all motivated to do something to help others. They recognized the suffering in those videos, and they were motivated to do something to alleviate it."

I told Dale about the reactions I would get from audiences when I spoke about Maurice and me. Most of the time, I could hear gasps when I talked about Maurice's terrible living conditions as a child, and sniffles when I described his beautiful family today. It was as if the crowd as a whole was reacting *physically* to our story. I told Dale how I could literally *feel* their energy and their emotions as they listened to me speak.

"This is the kindness contagion," Dale said. "If you put physiological monitors on everyone in that audience, you would see very real changes in how they were feeling and reacting. And if you talked to them afterward, they would tell you that they felt a tingling in their bodies. Think about how, when someone tells us something emotional, our hands go to our hearts. Our reaction is real and physical. And it's contagious."

In our talk, Dale also mentioned a book called *Rambam's Ladder: A Meditation on Generosity and Why It Is Necessary to Give* by Julie Salamon. The way Dale explained it, Rambam's Ladder refers to the eight rungs of giving described by a twelfth-century Jewish scholar named Maimonides (also known as Rambam). These eight rungs form a ladder that goes from the lowest degrees of virtue at the bottom—giving begrudgingly, giving too little—to the highest—giving whatever it takes to help someone else become self-reliant.

"It is a hierarchy of giving," Dale said, "and certain acts of giving bring you closer to God."

But here is the good news: research has shown that no matter what rung of the ladder you're on, as long as you are giving to others, you can experience *the same helper's high.*

"The act of giving itself can be very small," said Dale. "If you can go to Africa to help, God love you, by all means go. And if you're Bill Gates and you want to eradicate all disease, go for it. But most of us don't have those kinds of means."

And yet, "Every single one of us can hold a door open for someone else. All of us can catch someone's eye in the street and smile. All of us can say, 'Hey, that color is perfect on you.' Or on a playground, every kid can say, 'Why don't you come and play with us?'"

And then Dale said something that took me right back to Avital's school project—to her reference to *tikkun olam,* the Jewish value of repairing the world. "By helping one person at a time," Dale said, "you *are* saving the world. You are saving the world by performing an act of kindness that accumulates on top of other acts, and leads to even more acts of kindness, and all of these acts together are changing the world."

For years, Dale has worked with and counseled children who have been abused. She has seen the terrible effects that evil actions can have on a child. She has worked with children who were so traumatized they refused to even leave their homes. But in almost all the cases, Dale noticed a particular factor that made a profound difference in the lives of these children.

"What made the difference for them was *one person*," Dale

said. "These children needed to have one person who cared about them, who believed in them. To someone in need, one person can make all the difference in the world."

~~≈≋≈~~

I was fascinated and heartened to learn that everything I'd experienced about kindness in my journey—its benefits, its ability to change lives, its natural exhibition in children—was backed up by science and research.

I knew about the helper's high and how powerful it is, but I hadn't known it had been the subject of scientific study for two decades. I *sensed* the reaction that Dale referred to as kindness contagion, but I hadn't been aware that it could be proven through physiological testing.

Still, the truth is that we don't *need* to know the science to understand these very real phenomena. All we need to do is perform a kind action and experience the feelings for ourselves.

That is why sharing stories about kindness—and encouraging others to tap into their compassion—is exactly what the world needs right now. "When we witness nothing but evil and harm, we feel powerless," Dale says. "We need to be presented with the opportunity to say, 'Hey, wait a minute, I *can* make a difference. We *are* people who can alleviate suffering. We *are* compassionate beings.' And when we have that opportunity and act on it, we realize that we are deeply connected to one another, and that connection feels good."

"It is this wonderful double whammy," Dale says. "An act of kindness not only stops us from feeling powerless, it also makes us feel power*ful*."

~~≈≋≈~~

PART FOUR
AWARENESS

Why do certain people come into our lives? Is it all chance and randomness? I don't think so. I've met too many people, and heard too many stories like the ones in this section, to believe everything's an accident. It's easier for me to believe that when people cross into our path, they are there for a reason. But it's up to us to figure out that reason, and the way we do that is by living with awareness. By asking: Why is this person suddenly in my life? What beautiful connection might this be?

THE FRIENDSHIP

They were both seven years old, and they were in the same second-grade class.

But otherwise, they were as different as different could be.

Susan was Jewish and grew up in a suburb. Barbara was Christian and from the inner city.

Susan was blonde, with curly locks. Barbara had dark braided hair other children would touch out of curiosity.

Susan had a colorful lunchbox that carried sandwiches her mother made for her. Barbara had no lunchbox and ate a free lunch at school.

Susan was cheerful, outgoing, chatty. Barbara hardly spoke at all.

Susan and Barbara—two little girls from two different worlds.

How could they possibly be friends?

⁂

One of the beautiful things about invisible threads is how pure and innocent they are.

On my journey, I have seen these threads bring together all kinds of people—people you'd never think would cross paths. Old and young, rich and poor, timid and fearless—invisible threads cut through all divisions. That's because the things that are common to us all far outnumber the things that separate us.

As we grow up and get older, this simple lesson starts to fade. We become more skeptical, more jaded, less trusting. We pay more attention to what's different than to what is common. Our lives get cluttered and overly complicated.

Which is why I like to think of the world in terms of invisible threads.

Invisible threads connect people. They do not connect classes or races or ethnicities or religions or social cliques or income levels. They bind people by the heart, not by a zip code. They are always pure and innocent, even when we aren't anymore.

I'd heard about Susan and Barbara's story from Susan, who is a dear friend and a former colleague at *People*. But I didn't know their full story until after I started on my invisible thread journey. Only then did I realize what a beautiful illustration it is of how pure and powerful invisible thread connections can be.

When Susan Sagan Levitan was seven and first saw Barbara walk into her classroom at the Thornell Road Elementary School in Pittsford, New York, she was surprised. "I'd never seen a black person before in my life, except on TV," she says. "I lived in a very sheltered world."

Barbara Campbell had a similar reaction. "I was the only African American child in the room," she recalls. "It was very uncomfortable. They were all looking at me, and I was like, 'I don't want to be here.'"

Something called the Urban-Suburban Interdistrict Transfer Program brought them together. The program's goal was to racially integrate classrooms, but Susan and Barbara were way too young to understand any of that. "One day my mother just said, 'You're going to a new school,'" Barbara says. "I wasn't happy about it. When I got to the school, I thought that if I didn't talk, they would think I had comprehension problems and send me back to my old school. People would ask me questions, and I would just stare at them."

There was nothing wrong with Barbara, other than the feeling that she was alone in an unfamiliar place. Still, because she was so quiet, Barbara's teacher sent her to see a learning specialist. The specialist told her she could pick one classmate to come with her.

Barbara picked Susan.

It wasn't a hard choice. Up until then, none of her new class-mates had dared to talk to her, except for bubbly little Susan.

"We'd sit in a circle on the rug on the floor, and I would always save a seat for Barbara," Susan remembers. "I'd say, 'You can sit here, next to me.' I just felt connected to her from the very begin-ning. As different as we were, I just liked her."

After just one session with the learning specialist, Barbara was sent back to the regular class—and she and Susan quickly be-came close friends. "I'd get to school in the morning and look for her, and she would look for me," Barbara says. "We'd giggle and laugh, and we had our little secrets and inside jokes." Says Susan: "We'd run around the playground and have lunch together, and I remember telling my parents about her. I kept asking my mother, 'Can Barbara come over, please?'"

They had many play dates at Susan's home, and their friend-ship expanded beyond school. "Her parents were so nice to me, they didn't even seem real," Barbara says. "They'd ask, 'Who wants snacks? What do you want for dinner?' I wasn't used to that."

Then the two friends asked for a sleepover at Susan's house. Susan's mother agreed, but at first Barbara's mother said no. In Barbara's world, there simply weren't a lot of interactions with white people. "Most of the white people we saw were school principals and police officers," she says. "So when you saw some-one white it usually meant you were in trouble."

Fortunately, Barbara's mother worked with one of Susan's cousins, which helped her feel more comfortable. "Oh, I begged my mother to let me sleep over with Susan," Barbara recalls. "Fi-nally our mothers talked on the phone, and my mother let me go."

They had so much fun on their sleepover they decided they wanted another one, this time at Barbara's house. "She lived in a tough neighborhood," Susan remembers. "My parents were a little worried, but they knew it was the right thing to let me go." They drove Susan to Barbara's house, her little Raggedy Ann suitcase in tow, and dropped her off for the weekend. "It was this yellow house, and there were all these streetlights and sirens and this loud music coming from a bar across the street," Susan says. "We had pizza for dinner and then we all piled into one bed, me and Barbara and her sister. It was all so new to me."

When her mother picked her up, Susan was crying.

She was crying because she didn't want to leave.

"Mom, Barbara's house is the most beautiful house I've ever been in!" she said. "That was the best weekend of my life!"

Barbara's mother planned a perfect weekend for the girls. "She baked sweet potato pie with me, and she took us all to the zoo on a city bus," Susan remembers. "It was the first time I'd ever been on a bus and I loved it."

Barbara and Susan were friends for all of second grade and all of third grade. But on the first day of fourth grade, Susan looked around for her friend and couldn't find her. "I waited and waited for her, but she just never came," Susan says. "She had an older brother and sister in the school, and they weren't there, either.

She just vanished, and I was so confused. No one ever told me what happened."

In fact, Barbara's mother had decided to send her to live with her father in Alabama. "It happened so fast," Barbara says. "I never got a chance to say goodbye to Susan. My father came to pick me up, and I was gone."

The two friends missed each other. They often thought about each other. After a while they even began looking for each other.

But they never found each other.

Not for the next thirty-five years.

⁓

And just as their lives had run on different paths before they met, their lives veered off in different directions once again.

After high school, Susan attended the S.I. Newhouse School of Public Communications in Syracuse and graduated with honors. Then she left her small, sleepy hometown and moved to New York City. She got an apartment with a view of Central Park and the Empire State Building and started a career in the media industry, working in advertising sales at magazines like *People*, *New York*, and *Vanity Fair*. She ate at the best restaurants, went to Broadway premieres, met people like Oprah Winfrey, and worked out at the gym next to John F. Kennedy, Jr.

Her life, everyone would say, was like the show *Sex and the City*—and people on the street even stopped her to ask if she was Sarah Jessica Parker.

For Barbara, the path was rockier.

"My mother had five kids and was working twelve hours a day," she says. "She'd leave when I got up and come back when I was in bed. She tried her best to handle it all, but it was overwhelming for her. She just couldn't give us what we needed."

In the end, neither her father or her mother could take care of her. Barbara spent eight months in a youth detention center, and after that was placed in foster care. Then she wound up in a group home for teenagers. Finally, her mother petitioned a judge to make Barbara an emancipated minor. She was only sixteen years old. "I remember crying in the courtroom," she says. "I didn't even know what emancipation was. The judge asked me a couple of questions and said I was free to go."

Yet while Barbara and Susan were on different paths, they weren't completely separate from each other. That's because their brief friendship had already made its mark on them both.

Susan's life was filled with adventures, but in a way one of her first adventures was her time with Barbara. "She really opened my eyes to many things," Susan says. "She made me look at the world in a different way. She helped me be open to new people and new things."

Meanwhile, Barbara never forgot her boisterous friend, and thought of her often during her darkest times.

After being emancipated, Barbara stayed with her sisters. She learned she was pregnant, and she was determined to get her degree before her child was born. So she began studying for the GED. "The day of the test I had really bad morning sickness, so I put my head down on the cafeteria table and took the test like that," she says. Weeks later, she called a test official to get her results.

"Well," the official told her, "you got a perfect score on pretty much every section."

It took a lot of hard work, squeezed around several part-time and full-time jobs, but Barbara eventually graduated college and earned *two* associate degrees, in accounting and business administration.

"I made it on the dean's list," Barbara says. "When they handed me my diploma my son Vincent was in the audience yelling, 'That's my mom! That's my mom!' He was so proud of me."

Through it all, Barbara never stopped thinking about Susan. She didn't realize how much of an impact her friend had had on her until she went to a holiday office party and heard someone singing the Hanukkah song, "I Have a Little Dreidel." Suddenly, she found herself singing along. "I was the only one who knew all the words!" she says. "I was so surprised I knew them! And it was because Susan and her family included me in their holiday."

Over the years Barbara often tried to find Susan. One time, she was working as a telemarketer and saw the name of Susan's mother on the call list. "Susan's sister Amy answered, and I tried to explain to her who I was," Barbara says. "But she thought I was just trying to sell her something, so she hung up." Susan, too, tried to find her friend. "I'd look her up in phone books, but there are a thousand Barbara Campbells out there," she says. "And then one day, totally out of the blue, I got a Facebook friend request."

It was April 2014. The request was from Barbara Campbell.

"First," Barbara explains, "I found someone else who had been in the Urban-Suburban program, and I saw on her page that she had liked something on Susan's sister's page. Then I clicked on her list of friends, and there was Susan's name. I was so excited, I screamed."

Barbara sent the friend request and waited. A day passed. Two days passed. A third day passed. "I was so anxious," she says. "I thought, 'My life has been so crazy, and she's probably not going to want to associate with me.'"

She couldn't have been more wrong.

When Susan finally saw the friend request, she immediately accepted and sent a private message.

LAURA SCHROFF

"Hello there!!" she wrote. "It's been a LONG time. Hope you are doing well. I remember how much fun we used to have together."

They messaged back and forth for a long time. After that they exchanged emails and phone calls and finally agreed to meet for lunch at The Cheesecake Factory in Rochester.

Before the lunch, both of the old friends were nervous. Would they still like each other? Would they have anything to talk about anymore?

"I got to the restaurant first, and I stood near the front, waiting," Susan recalls. "And the second she walked in, I knew it was her."

"I was so scared, but then we hugged and we both got teary-eyed, and you know what? She was the same person!" Barbara says. "The exact same person! Same sweet personality and caring heart. She was just . . . Susan."

They filled each other in on their lives. They laughed and talked about the old days. They traded happy memories—having fun with a Magic 8 Ball, jumping rope, playing hopscotch.

Then they decided to visit their second-grade classroom together.

"It was amazing," Susan says. "It was like stepping into a time machine. Everything was the same as it had been, except it looked so little. We were like, 'This is where we sat together! And this is where we used to play!' We remembered every little place we used to go together—the front office, the cafeteria, the library."

Says Barbara: "It all came flooding back. I looked at the tiny little chairs and remembered how we always wanted to be together. Our names were far apart alphabetically, but we always asked to sit together. That's all we ever wanted."

As fate would have it, Susan and Barbara are together again, at least geographically. After more than twenty years in Manhattan, Susan—with her husband, Michael, and their two beautiful sons, Zach and Max—made the bittersweet decision to leave the city she loves so much and move back to Rochester. Barbara is in Rochester, too, working as an administrative clerk. They talk on the phone and text each other often, usually after 9:00 p.m., when Susan's children are asleep.

"Our friendship had a big impact on me," Susan says. "It was so special and out of the ordinary. We had no reason in the world to connect. But we did. We just did. We were innocent, and we liked each other. We didn't know how different we were."

"It's hard to explain, but we just have this incredible connection," Barbara adds. "I still feel like I can talk to Susan about anything. We took a photo together at The Cheesecake Factory that day, and sometimes I just look at it in disbelief. I honestly thought I'd never see Susan again."

But whatever wonderful force brought them together in the first place, all those years ago, finally brought them together again.

"We had this crazy little sisterhood that no one understood but us, and that will never change," says Barbara. "Not today, and not in another thirty-five years."

RIGHT PERSON, RIGHT PLACE, RIGHT TIME

A good friend sent me a newspaper story about a twelve-year-old Utah boy named Matthew.

One day, Matthew asked his local mailman if he had any extra junk mail. The mailman was perplexed and asked the boy why he wanted junk mail. Matthew's explanation: he loved reading, but his family was too poor to afford a car, or even bus fare, so he couldn't get to the library. The only thing he had to read was junk mail.

The mailman, Ron Lynch, quickly shared the story on his Facebook page and asked people to send Matthew books. He expected a handful to trickle in.

Instead, Matthew wound up with more than five hundred books.

The story of Ron and Matthew is a great example of what happens when we live our lives with awareness. Because when we accept that the connections between us aren't simply random, we're likely to discover that sometimes, we are just the right person in just the right place at just the right time.

Which, really, is all an angel on earth is.

Right person, right place, right time.

15

THE FIRST WORD

Lou Honderich grew up and lived in the heart of the country—Tulsa, Oklahoma. She and her husband, Jeff, a family practice physician, had four children and a perpetually noisy home. But even so, Lou and her husband both felt they'd like to have another little one in the house. That's when Lou, a former kindergarten teacher, saw a TV news report about the desperate need for foster parents. "That was it," Lou says. "I knew fostering was for us. I felt we'd been blessed with four beautifully healthy children, and I always felt so fortunate, and part of that was wanting to help others who weren't so lucky."

She got her chance almost immediately, when a little boy who was in foster care across the street came over to her house to say hi.

"How old are you?" she asked him one day.

"Five," the boy said.

"Oh, I love that age," Lou said.

"Well, I bet you could have me if you wanted me, 'cause they don't like me in my home," the boy replied.

Lou dug around and discovered the boy's foster family arrangement wasn't ideal. In fact, the family planned to take a summer trip to Disneyland without the boy and asked Lou to babysit him while they were gone.

"He was a street kid, very brash and a little mouthy," Lou says.

"His foster parents didn't know what to do with him. But he became my little buddy. I'd fix him snacks, and he hung out with my kids, and he fit right in."

The boy's caseworker took notice, and Lou and Jeff became his official foster parents for the next few weeks, until he went back to his mother and father. Another little boy followed, and Lou fostered him for two years. "He was only two when he came to us," she says. "His parents had problems with drugs and had lived on the streets and in shelters. He was so fascinated with everything in our home. He would walk around and just touch the drapes, like he couldn't believe windows could have drapes."

Eventually, another couple adopted the boy. "We wanted to adopt him, but they gave preference to a couple that had no children," Lou recalls. "It was heartbreaking to let him go. I remember one of my own kids saying, 'How could you let them take my baby brother away?'"

Late one afternoon, Lou got a call from a caseworker. The worker's voice was urgent. "You need to go to the hospital tomorrow," she told Lou. "We have a little girl there who needs you."

Because Jeff was a physician, Lou often found herself fostering children with special medical needs. That's why she got the call about the little girl. "They told me she was refusing to eat," Lou says. "She was tiny. The nurses in the hospital just didn't have the time to help her. So they needed someone to feed her."

Lou eventually learned the details of the girl's situation. Her parents were extremely poor and also inexperienced with children. When the little girl was one, she was switched straight from formula to regular milk and food. Her parents didn't give her baby food or gradually introduce her to solid foods. The girl had a severe gag reflex and threw up everything. The parents saw it as a discipline problem and tried to force her to eat. That only made matters worse.

Now the girl was in the hospital, critically malnourished. She was also emotionally closed off and hadn't spoken a single word since arriving.

Lou drove to the hospital the next morning after dropping her kids off at school. She walked into a large room where two little boys were playing. She saw the little girl—Erica—off by herself, staring at nothing. "She was twenty months old and probably weighed only fourteen pounds," Lou says. "She was so underweight, and she had a distended stomach. But, oh, my goodness, she was darling. She had such beautiful dark hair and this pretty face. She was a little angel."

Erica had what doctors called a flat affect—no expression, no engagement, no recognition of other people. If anyone tried to touch her—particularly men—she recoiled. "They flew her to the hospital in a helicopter, and when a male resident tried to examine her, she became hysterical," Lou says. "They had to wait for a female physician to come on duty." And no matter what food Erica was given, she just refused to eat. "The problem was she didn't know *how* to eat," says Lou. "No one had taught her how to chew."

Lou realized immediately that the nurses were doing their best. But they had other patients and not enough time to give Erica special treatment. What's more, they could only use the hospital's toddler menu, which included a lot of crunchy foods such as tacos and carrot sticks. As a result, Erica shut down. "When I walked in, the little boys ran right over to me," says Lou. "Erica didn't."

Instinctively, Lou knew what to do. Before she even tried to feed her anything, she first had to gain her trust. Lou picked up a children's book and said, "Who wants to hear a story?" Both boys shouted yes; Erica didn't budge. Then Lou asked, "Who wants to sit in my lap while I read?" One of the little boys jumped right up into Lou's lap; again, Erica didn't budge.

Then Lou turned her chair away from Erica. Not toward her— *away*.

"I didn't want her to be able to see the book I was reading," Lou explains. "I knew that she would want to see the pictures I was describing, and I wanted her to get up and come close to me."

Lou read the children a story, but still, Erica didn't budge.

Lou picked up another book to read and sat the second boy in her lap. This time, she turned her chair slightly so Erica could see the book. When she started reading, Erica stood up and leaned in so she could see the pictures, too.

Then Lou took a chance.

When she finished the second book, she picked up a third and turned to the tiny little girl.

"Erica, do you want to sit on my lap while I read this one?" Lou asked.

Moments passed. Erica stood there, frozen.

Then, slowly, she reached out her arms and stretched them toward Lou. Lou scooped her up and placed her gently in her lap.

After the third story, it was lunchtime. The nurses brought in more hard food. Lou asked if they could persuade the kitchen to send up applesauce and a mashed banana. After a while, the nurses came back with the soft food. Lou brought her chair near Erica and, with a small spoon, offered her some of the applesauce.

"She was hesitant, but she ate some off the spoon," Lou says. "I gave her another little bit and she ate that, too. She had a few more little bites and then she turned away, and I didn't push it. But after I fed her I held her in my lap for a while, so her stomach would be settled."

The arrangement had been for Lou to help feed Erica lunch, not dinner. So that afternoon, she said goodbye to all the children and went back home. The next morning, when she came back, one of the nurses told her Erica had refused to eat any dinner.

Lou walked into the room where the children were and looked to see if Erica would have any reaction to her.

"She was still pretty much the same," Lou says, "but I thought I saw a tiny little ghost of a smile."

Lou read more stories and fed Erica soft food again. This time, she ate a little more. Lou left the hospital after lunch but came back again in the evening after she'd made dinner for her family. "I didn't want to give her baby food because she wasn't a baby," Lou says. "I asked the nurses if they could bring up some mashed potatoes, and I fed her little spoonfuls of that." Before she left, she cradled Erica in her lap again and sang her a song to get her ready for bed. "I could hold her now," says Lou. "But she still hadn't said a word."

On their third day together, Lou showed up at the hospital in the morning, same as the first two days. When she walked into the children's room, she looked for any reaction from Erica.

This time, Erica stood up, looked at Lou, and, in the barest, tiniest whisper of a voice, uttered a single word: "Mama."

"The nurses couldn't believe it," says Lou. "We were all so surprised. And right at that moment, when she said that one little word, I was bound to this child forever. It happened so fast, and it was such an intense connection. It felt almost *spiritual*."

Lou and Erica continued their routine for several days. A doctor believed it would benefit Erica if she were moved from the hospital to a home, so Lou and Jeff became Erica's foster parents. "She was still frightened of men, and here were my husband and two teenage boys, all of them really tall. But for whatever reason, Erica was never afraid of my guys. Not the least bit afraid."

At home, Lou stepped up Erica's feedings from three a day to five a day. It took nearly two years, but Erica finally caught up in height and weight to other children her age. Lou also took her to speech therapy. She still said "mama" all the time, but she started to add other words, too.

Erica's biological parents eventually gave up their parental rights, and the Honderichs began the process to adopt her. When Erica was five, she asked if she could have a new name. Lou let her pick out a new middle name and gave her a list of names to choose from.

"Can I be named for someone?" she asked.

"Of course you can," Lou said.

"Well, can I be named for Jesus Christ? Wasn't he the most important person ever?"

"Yes, he was," Lou said.

And so she picked Christine—which is what everyone calls her today.

When the adoption was finalized, Erica officially became part of Lou's family. "But the truth," Lou says, "is that she was always ours."

~≈~

Christine is all grown up now, with a good job and a loving husband. She lives one town over from Lou, and they see each other all the time. "She once said to me, 'If you had told me when I was a teenager that the one person I would most want to have lunch with is my mother, I would have told you, you were crazy,'" Lou says with a laugh. "But that's how she feels. She said, 'Mom, you will always come first for me.'"

Lou doesn't know what Christine's future would have been had she not entered the picture. Better? Worse? It's impossible to say.

But even so, says Lou, "I am convinced she needed to be with us. A few weeks before I met her, I began having this dream about a young girl coming into my life. Now, all of my kids have blonde hair, but in my dreams this little girl had beautiful dark hair. I had no idea where this toddler with the dark hair came from, or who she was supposed to be. But I kept dreaming about her. Now I know that Christine and I were connected before we ever met."

Was it fate? The universe's master plan? How can two people be connected before they even meet?

Lou feels an invisible thread is as good a name for it as any. "I do believe we are drawn toward what we need in life," she says. "We needed Christine, and she needed us, and luckily we found each other. Whatever you want to call it, that is a very special, very beautiful thing."

A) OR B)

"We are drawn toward what we need in life"—what a beautiful sentiment. It implies a world that doesn't have to be seen as chaotic and random. It implies a kind of universal force, operating behind the scenes, that brings order and meaning to our lives. I believe in this force—I believe we are drawn to the people who need us, and to the people we need.

The day I first met Maurice in 1986 was a Monday, which should have been a workday but was actually Labor Day. Instead of going to work, I had tickets to attend the U.S. Open tennis tournament in Flushing Meadows, New York.

But the day began with pouring rain, which washed out the tournament. My backup plan was to stay inside all day and catch up on paperwork and phone calls. Had it continued to rain, I almost certainly wouldn't have left my apartment.

But the rain stopped and the sun came out.

And only then did I decide to go for a walk to stretch my legs and get some air. Normally, my work schedule was so packed I didn't have time for pleasant little strolls—and certainly not in the middle of a weekday. It just so happened that on that day, I did. When I left my apartment, I could have taken a right turn and walked on Eighth Avenue. Instead, for no particular reason, I took a left turn and walked down Broadway.

And walked right into Maurice.

The holiday. The rain. The canceled tournament. The late-breaking sun. The left turn. All of that had to happen exactly the way it happened, or else I never would have met Maurice—and I'd never have found one of the great blessings of my life.

Coincidence? Happenstance? Just a random collision of two people?

I guess some people will say that.

But not me.

I might have agreed with the "coincidence" argument back when I met Maurice, and maybe even just a few years ago.

But all the people I've met and all the stories I've heard over the last five years have forever changed and expanded my view of how the world works.

So how about you?

What do you think it was that brought Maurice and me together?

A) Pure dumb luck, or

B) Fate, destiny, invisible threads—whatever you want to call the universal force that draws people who need each other together.

Now here's the interesting thing—there is no right answer. There's no way to prove either A or B is correct. It all comes down to what we choose to believe about the world we live in. And what we choose to believe about the world dictates how we live in it.

That is what I mean by awareness. It means being aware of what you believe to be true about the workings of the world. Having a definitive view of how and why things happen.

So go ahead. Think about it. Then decide which answer makes more sense to you.

16

THE HURRICANE

It started as a tropical wave in the Atlantic Ocean.

It moved north and gained strength and slammed into Puerto Rico. Within two days it was a full-blown hurricane, its winds a devastating 120 mph. By the time it hit New York's Long Island in late August 2011, it had weakened a bit. But it was still deadly, and it caused massive flooding, power outages in 350,000 homes, and ten deaths. Hurricane Irene was the most destructive storm to reach New York in forty years.

And in the middle of it all was Linda Preuss.

Linda is a lovely, cheerful woman now in her sixties. When she was forty-eight, after many years of feeling inexplicably tired, she underwent a spinal tap; the test revealed she had multiple sclerosis, an often disabling disease of the central nervous system. "It was a pretty quick decline from there," says her daughter, Jessica, a store window designer. "Over four or five years she basically lost all mobility. By the time I graduated from college, she was in a wheelchair."

Linda, who was divorced, lived by herself in a ground-floor apartment in Massapequa, Long Island, just a few yards from a canal. She hired a series of aides to help her, but most of them weren't helpful at all. Some stole from her; others simply walked out on her. She also didn't have any friends she could talk to about her MS. At times, her life was lonely and difficult.

Then the hurricane came.

The canal near where Linda lived overflowed, and two feet of water flooded into her small apartment. Because she was in a wheelchair, Linda could not get through the water by herself. Luckily, a team of volunteers helped evacuate her and took her to a nearby emergency shelter. There, another volunteer carried Linda from place to place and kept her safe and dry.

Linda never learned the names of these volunteers. They just appeared during a crisis and performed lifesaving acts of kindness.

Finally, Linda was taken to a hospital, where she stayed for a few days. Someone there asked her where she wanted to go next.

"I'd heard about a place called the Hamptons Center, where they had some people with MS," Linda says. "I told them I wanted to go there."

Tom Grotticelli was fourteen years old when he started feeling like something was wrong. Six years later, he was diagnosed with MS. "I lost mobility and had to use a wheelchair," he says. "It went into remission for five years, then came back. I have had the disease for fifty years now."

Tom, a computer programmer who is divorced, was living with an aide in a home on Long Island. One day, his aide announced she was quitting. "She said, 'That's it, I can't take it anymore. I'm done,'" Tom recalls. "She took me to the hospital and left me in my wheelchair at the curb. I had to ask someone to push me inside."

It was a painful and desperate time for Tom. He had spent his savings on hiring aides, paying for his boarding, and buying a wheelchair-accessible van. "I was destitute," he says. "I felt like

I was at the very end of the road." Hospital officials and social workers met with his aide, hoping she might reconsider, but she didn't. Tom was suddenly a man without a home.

But the hospital officials and social workers didn't give up on him. They worked with him to make sure he had a comfortable place to go.

"I'd heard about a place from the MS Society, where they had some MS patients," Tom says. "I asked some of the patients who lived there if it was a nice place, and if they liked living there, and they said they did." His social worker called the nursing home and found they had an open bed.

"So I said, 'Okay, send me there,'" Tom remembers. "And that's where they sent me."

It was another act of kindness during a crisis that delivered Tom to the Hamptons Center.

One day at the center, Tom was in his wheelchair by the nurses' station when he noticed a woman out of the corner of his eye.

"All I remember thinking is, 'She is so pretty,'" Tom says. "I was sitting there where everyone hangs out, and I just spoke up. I said, 'Hi, I'm Tom.' And she said, 'Hi, I'm Linda.'"

"He was very easy to talk to," remembers Linda. "I thought he was kind of good-looking. I didn't mind talking to him at all."

After that first meeting, Tom made a point to talk to Linda every day.

"I'd come out and when I'd see her I'd yell, 'Linda!'" he says. "I would yell really loudly across the room so she wouldn't miss me."

Since then, Tom and Linda have been inseparable. Jessica says, "When I'd come to visit, all the aides and nurses would be fawning over their relationship. Tom didn't have an automated wheelchair, so my mother let him hold on to the back of her wheelchair and pulled him around."

"Until the social worker said I couldn't do that anymore," adds Tom. "Too dangerous."

Finally, Tom and Linda had someone they could talk to about their MS—someone who understood what they were going through. But they didn't just talk about the disease; they talked about *everything*. Their lives, their marriages, their children, their favorite shows. "Then we asked if we could live in the same room," Tom says. "At first they weren't sure, but then they said they were okay with it, so we moved in together."

Eventually Linda told Tom about her difficult experiences with health care aides. He told her his aide had abandoned him at a curb.

"When he told me that, I just felt so bad for him," Linda recalls. "So I said, 'Okay, let's find a place to live together.'"

Tom thought that was a great idea. "From then," he says, "we were both dedicated to getting out of the nursing home."

But getting out wasn't as easy as they thought.

There were many obstacles in the way of Tom and Linda finding a place to be together. For one thing, they had very specific needs. They needed an apartment that was wheelchair accessible and also had a roll-in shower. "We looked all over for something that worked for us," Tom says. "We went on the Web and looked at places and asked people for help. It was hard, but we kept at it."

They finally found an apartment in a retirement community that was perfect. They submitted a down payment and began packing their things. On the day of the move their boxes were loaded into a van, and Tom and Linda wheeled through the lobby, saying goodbye to their friends.

Then, at the last minute, a social worker stopped them.

"I'm sorry," she said, "but you can't leave."

There was a problem. Before Hurricane Irene, Linda had lived in one Long Island county, and now she wanted to move to a different county. Medicare regulations, however, blocked her from doing that. "They insisted she had to live by herself for a month before moving," Jessica says. "I had to get on the phone and talk to Medicare officials and social workers and county officers for hours. *Hundreds* of hours."

Then, one day, there was good news—Tom and Linda were told the paperwork was in order, and they could finally go. They packed up the van once more and prepared to leave.

But at the last minute, they were stopped again. Another paperwork problem.

"It became impossible for us to leave," says Linda. "This went on for months and months."

Still, they never gave up hope. They had made it through worse. Being abandoned. A hurricane. A disabling disease. They were not going to let a bureaucratic brick wall stand in their way.

It took six months—and a heroic effort by Jessica—but eventually the brick wall came down. Medicare cleared the move, and Linda and Tom were free to leave and start their new lives. "It was wonderful," Linda says. "The community where we live now is large and open and has waterfalls when you come in. And when the weather is nice, there's a place we can go outside and sit together."

Tom says, "Sometimes we'll go to a restaurant. And we like to go to shows. *Mummenschanz*, we went to that a couple of months ago. Most of the time, we'll just hold hands. We hold hands all the time."

Last Christmas, Tom bought a beautiful ring for Linda—crushed diamonds with white gold and rose gold hearts. The next February, Linda was taken to the hospital with pneumonia, and her daughter rushed to see her. "I walked in and said, 'How are you? How are you doing?'" Jessica remembers. "And all she said was, 'Look at the ring Tom got me!' She was beaming."

"Now," Linda adds, "I never take it off."

Linda never expected something like this to happen to her. "Oh, no, never," she says. "I thought, 'I am in a wheelchair; no one is going to love me now.'" Tom, too, had all but given up on happiness. "I didn't think I'd ever meet anyone," he says. "Not at my age, not with all the things that happened to me."

And yet they've been together for four years now, two of those in their new home. "It has been amazing," says Jessica. "I can see how much of a difference it has made in my mother's life. She found someone who can relate to her, and now she doesn't need to call me all the time. It gives me so much relief and happiness to see them together. Out of such a terrible nightmare, something beautiful happened."

And now, no matter what obstacles arise, Tom and Linda plan on staying together forever.

"Me and Tom, we love each other," Linda says. "I'm so happy I'm with him."

"I fell in love with Linda the minute I saw her," says Tom. "Being with her has given me a whole new life. Linda is everything to me."

The woman made homeless by a hurricane and the man

abandoned at a hospital—brought together by separate acts of kindness.

United, you could say, by angels.

"I do believe certain people are meant to be together," Linda says.

"Me, too," says Tom, holding Linda's hand. "It was destiny."

GRACE IN CHAOS

Before I began my invisible thread journey and heard the story of Tom and Linda, I hadn't realized that even the darkest moments of our lives are actually opportunities for grace.

Grace is defined as a bestowal of blessings, and that's what happened to Tom and Linda. Thanks to the efforts of several angels on earth, they found a great blessing in the wake of a hurricane and an unexpected displacement. Somehow their darkest moments became their brightest time.

Angels on earth find grace in chaos.

I wasn't always able to see the silver linings in my life, but today I always look for grace in the chaos. I'm always aware that kindness and compassion can turn even the worst setback into something beautiful.

17

THE TWINS

Nancy Kropacek sent me an email that was really about two stories—the story of Yvonne Ann, and the story of the twins.

Nancy grew up in the South, and her parents were smart and civic-minded. They protested in support of civil rights in the 1960s and taught their four children the value of looking out for others. When Nancy grew up, she went to live at a spiritual community called the Farm in rural Tennessee. It was there, in 1975, that she gave birth to her first daughter, Irene Elizabeth, on a beautiful starry night. Two years later, she was pregnant again, but this time, something went wrong.

Her abdomen was abnormally enlarged. She was so big, people assumed she was having twins. In fact, she was retaining too much water. She went into labor, and twenty-three difficult hours later, her daughter Yvonne Ann was born. "She was absolutely beautiful," Nancy wrote in her email. "I was so thrilled to welcome her into the world."

But right from the start, Yvonne Ann was having trouble breathing. She was rushed to a hospital, where a team of cardiac doctors took over her care. After a few hours, several doctors came out and sat down with Nancy and her husband.

"They told us that our beautiful sweet angel was not going

to survive," Nancy wrote. "It felt as if someone had ripped my heart out." Nancy went in to see her infant daughter one last time and found her hooked up to tubes and machines. "I told her how much I loved her, and how sorry I was that she would not get to be here with me. Then my whole body collapsed. I screamed and cried and screamed. Grief, guilt, and sadness flooded over me. I cried for days and days, and I prayed to God to help me heal and let me carry on."

Yvonne Ann passed away from congenital heart disease, which ran in Nancy's family. Her angel was on this earth for only five hours.

They held a funeral for Yvonne Ann at the Farm. "It was just this little ceremony, and someone read scriptures, and everyone was there to support me and pray for her," Nancy says. "But the truth is, I can't remember much about the funeral. I was in total shock. All I remember is the crushing grief. I felt this terrible emptiness, this *absence*. I was expecting a child, and then suddenly the child wasn't there."

Nancy was still in deep mourning when, two weeks later, a midwife at the Farm approached her with a question.

"We heard about a young mother who just gave birth to twins and cannot keep them," the midwife said. "Would you be interested in caring for them?"

The Farm was known for taking in infants and children who needed temporary homes. The community was a kind of big, unofficial foster family. No sooner had the midwife finished her question than Nancy heard herself utter a single word: "Yes."

"I didn't even think about it," she says now. "It was all instinct. I knew these twins needed me, and I knew they would help me heal. My only concern was my daughter Irene, but she was all for it. And so, that's what happened."

The twins had been born two months prematurely to a twenty-one-year-old college student named Mary. Mary had been expecting one seven-pound baby; instead, there were two infants, one weighing 3.6 pounds, the other 3.2. Mary was excited to be a mother, but she had no parents or close relatives who could help with care or money, and raising her twins all alone was overwhelming. "She just wasn't ready for them," Nancy says. Yet Mary was adamant about one thing—she didn't want to give the twins up for adoption, because that meant they would likely be separated. "She had heard about the Farm," Nancy says, "so she brought the twins to us."

Something was made clear to Nancy from the start: There was a possibility the mother might not ever come back for her twins. But there was also the possibility she might.

It was Mary who brought the twins—Eliza and Rose—to the Farm and handed them over to Nancy. "They were in blankets, and they were so tiny," she remembers. Nancy had been prepared to nurse her own daughter, which meant she was also ready to begin nursing the twins right away. "That really made a difference," she says. "They started getting a little chunk to them."

Nancy's connection to the twins was instant and intense. "I fell in love with them the second I held them," she says. "They were so small and sweet. I could easily tell them apart, and I had them figured out immediately. Eliza was the quiet one, while Rose was feisty and energetic. And that's how they were with me."

Weeks passed, then months, then a year. Nancy stopped thinking of herself as a caretaker to the twins, because that's not how she felt inside. "They absolutely felt like my own children," she says. "I had to do everything for them. Early on, the feedings were around the clock. And they needed a lot of extra attention. Thankfully, my daughter Irene loved them as much as I did and loved helping me take care of them."

One morning, a midwife on the Farm came to see Nancy again.

"She told me she'd received a call," says Nancy. "Mary was ready to take the twins back."

Mary had completed her education, started a full-time job, saved money, and set up her house for children. She was now ready for the twins. For Nancy, saying goodbye was painful. More than painful—impossible. "I knew they needed to be with their mother, but a part of me didn't want to give them up," she says. "It felt like the nightmare was happening again. I was grieving all over again."

Nancy tried to stay in touch with Eliza and Rose. She sent them cards on their birthday and toys for Christmas and little notes just to say hello. Once in a while their mother sent Nancy photos of the twins, too. They even arranged for Nancy to come visit the twins a year or so after they left the Farm, but "that meeting was really awkward," she says. "The girls didn't know what to think or what to do."

Still, Nancy kept writing, kept telling the twins how much she missed them. But time passed, and Nancy wrote them less frequently, and Mary sent fewer photos, and eventually they lost touch altogether. "I knew when their eighteenth birthday was, but I couldn't invite myself to be there," she says. "I knew when they were graduating high school, but I had to miss that, too."

Somewhere in that time, it occurred to Nancy that the twins had probably forgotten all about her. After all, they'd been only two years old when they were separated, and not many memories—if any—survive from that young age.

"How could such an intense relationship just cease to exist like that?" she wondered. "How could such a deep connection not leave any trace?"

Then, in 2010—thirty-three years after she'd said goodbye to the twins—the email came.

It was from Eliza.

"I have thought of you often the past few years," her note read. "I have now built up the courage to contact you. Thank you for taking such good care of my twin and me. I would love to know more about you."

Nancy erupted into tears on the spot.

"I saw her name pop up on my computer, and I couldn't believe it," she says. "I can't tell you what a wonderful, wonderful moment that was for me. To not be forgotten? To be remembered? That was *everything* to me."

They arranged to meet in a hotel in Miami, where Eliza was attending a conference. Nancy and her husband, Wally, waited anxiously in the lobby for Eliza to arrive. They hadn't seen each other in close to three decades—how would they even recognize each other? "Then I looked down the lobby and I saw a crowd of people coming, and Eliza was in the middle of the crowd," says Nancy. "I knew instantly it was her."

Then Eliza saw her and recognized her right away, too. "And then she came running at me," says Nancy, "and she jumped right in my arms."

Nancy cried. So did Eliza.

So did Wally, and so did the colleague who'd come with Eliza.

So did several other people in the lobby who didn't even know what was happening.

"We hugged for a long, long time," says Nancy. "I didn't want to let go."

They spent the evening together and sat by the hotel pool and talked into the wee hours. Eliza told Nancy that her twin sister Rose, too, was interested in meeting her, but that Rose needed to approach the meeting at her own pace. "Then she told me how thankful they both were for everything I'd done for them," says Nancy. "And I told her, 'No, you two helped *me*.' I told her about Yvonne Ann, and I told her how she and her sister had allowed me to heal."

Then Eliza said what she really came to say.

"It's because of you," she told Nancy, "that Rose and I got to stay together."

That was it. That was the answer to Nancy's question. *How could such a deep connection leave no trace?*

The answer was it *had* left a trace. It *had* made a difference—an *enormous* difference.

"Our lives wouldn't be the same if it weren't for you," Eliza told Nancy. "You changed our lives forever."

One invisible thread had preserved another—the thread between Eliza and Rose.

The next day, Eliza gave Nancy a present. It was a beautiful, white-and-black turquoise necklace. "She said she wanted me to have it because it sits close to the heart," Nancy says. "I still wear it every day."

Eliza stayed with Nancy and Wally at their home for a week. She saw Nancy's daughter Irene again, after thirty-three years, and they hit it off immediately. Finally, and sadly, it was time for Eliza to go home. "Even when she was here, it was hard for us to be apart," Nancy says. "It was *physically* difficult for us to separate—that's how profound the connection was. She didn't want to go, and I didn't want her to go." This time, though, they said goodbye knowing they'd see each other again.

Neither Eliza nor Rose had any actual memories of their time with Nancy. All they knew of her was what Mary had told them—that Nancy had cared for them and been like a mother to them.

That, nearly four decades earlier, Nancy had said yes to the twins—in the hour of her own greatest sadness.

And that is how an act of kindness connected not only Nancy and the twins, but also the twins and Yvonne Ann—the sweet little angel whose five hours on earth made a lifetime of difference to two girls she never even met.

Incredibly, Yvonne Ann and the twins even shared a due date: August 8.

"The twins didn't remember me, but that's okay, because the connection between us wasn't in the brain," Nancy says. "The connection between us was always in our hearts."

≈≈≈

SIGNS AND CUES

Be open and be aware—that has been my challenge to you.

To which you might have responded, "But how?"

How, exactly, do we know if we're connected to someone by an invisible thread? How can we tell if a moment is a turning point or just any old moment? Are we just supposed to guess when it's time to be an angel on earth?

Good questions.

I've thought a lot about why I came back to see Maurice on the corner of Broadway in 1986. As I've discussed many times, I initially walked right by him, but just a few seconds later, I stopped in my tracks. Here is how I described what happened next in my book: "And then— and I'm still not sure why I did this—I came back."

I wrote those words twenty-five years after meeting Maurice. Remarkably, in all that time, I still hadn't quite figured out what it was that made me go back to him.

Today, five years later, I believe I finally know.

In those five years, so many people have shared their stories with me, each with its own unique twist, each powerful in a different way. And all these stories have helped me understand my own story better— they have helped me figure out why I did what I did.

You see, nearly all of the stories include a beautiful moment when something mysterious and magical happens that changes the course of the action—a turning point moment.

And that mysterious and magical thing, I now understand, is a sign.

A sign is how we know when to act. Just like a directional sign on the side of a road, these signs steer us where we need to go. Living our lives with awareness means being on the lookout for these signs and recognizing them when they happen.

These signs can take many forms, most of which we already recognize. They can be a gut instinct. They can be intuition. They can be a voice in our head. A hunch, an urge, a premonition. A subconscious jab in the ribs.

Pay attention to the weird feelings you get in certain situations. Just as we are programmed to avoid dangerous situations—think of that surge of adrenaline that can make our stomach do flips—I believe we are also wired to seize opportunities for kindness. I believe we receive cues from the universe that pave the way for compassionate action.

Now, I wasn't aware that I was heeding a sign when I turned around and went back to Maurice in 1986. But if we become aware of these signs and cues and learn how to trust them, then our potential to be angels on earth increases greatly.

So why did I turn around and go back to Maurice? What was my sign or cue? I like the term a woman named Barbara Ginsberg used in her email to me. Barbara called it a tug.

———————————————————————————

18

THE TUG

Barbara's story begins back in 1979, when she was nineteen years old and working in a Pennsylvania mall.

"I was taking a break from college, and my mother told me I had to get a full-time job," she says. "I went into the mall and walked by every store, looking for HELP WANTED signs." She didn't see any and was about to leave, when a friend who worked in a kiosk selling jewelry asked her if she'd tried Pier 1. In fact, Barbara had walked past the store but hadn't seen the sign. "So I went back and interviewed and got the job," she says. "It was kind of random."

She was hired to work the day shift as a cashier for about four dollars an hour. Some evenings, when Barbara's shift was ending, she'd run into the nighttime cashier, a pretty, freckled, curly-haired redhead named Sue, then fifteen. They didn't work together, and only saw each other in passing.

As Sue remembers it, "We didn't really know each other. Barbara was leaving, I was coming, and maybe we'd say hello. I always thought of her as the quiet one."

All Barbara knew about Sue was that she had a bit of a reputation as a party girl. "When I started, someone told me, 'Oh, yeah, Sue, she's a handful,'" Barbara says. "I just thought of her as a typical fifteen-year-old, with the typical teenage angst."

Occasionally, Sue would tell Barbara about a wild night she'd had.

"One evening she came in and said, 'I must have had a really great time over the weekend, because my radio's broken, and I can't remember how I broke it,'" Barbara recalls. "And I thought, 'Wow, that can't be good that she can't remember.'"

One evening, Barbara was finishing up her shift and just about to leave when Sue walked in. Right away, Barbara noticed something was different.

"She was really down," Barbara says. "She told me she'd just broken up with her boyfriend. It wasn't like her usual complaints about her parents or whatever. It felt a lot heavier than that."

Then Sue said something that shocked her: "Life isn't worth it," Sue said. "I want to kill myself."

~~~~~

At first, Barbara didn't know if she should take her seriously or not. "It was surreal to hear her talk about suicide all of a sudden," she says. "I felt bad for her. I'd broken up with boyfriends before. But I didn't know how to take it. So I listened to her complain about how awful her life was for a while, then I left to go home."

Barbara headed for the mall exit, on the way to the parking lot. But after she'd taken just a few steps, she stopped.

"I turned on my heels," she remembers. "I turned around, and instead of walking to my car, I walked upstairs to a bookstore."

"My thought was, 'What do I do about Sue?'" she says. "But I was also thinking, 'Well, she's just a teenager.' I didn't really know what I was doing. All I knew was that if I was going to get Sue something, it had to be inexpensive because I didn't have much money."

Near the entrance of the B. Dalton bookstore, she saw a rack of feel-good books. "Pictures of cute animals, little inspirational quotes, books like that," she says. She settled on one called *How to Survive the Loss of a Love*. It was only about a hundred pages, and it was hugely popular at the time. "I thought it might be too heavy and serious for her, but when I looked through it, it felt right," she says. "So I took a chance and bought it."

Barbara returned to Pier 1 with the book in a paper bag. Sue looked up, surprised to see her.

"This is for you," Barbara said, handing her the book. "I hope you feel better."

Then she turned around, walked out, and went home.

Barbara didn't see Sue the next day; in fact, she didn't see her for a while. Not long after that, Barbara quit her job and moved to Connecticut.

"I never knew what happened with Sue," she says. "I just moved on."

<hr>

Nine years later, Barbara and her husband, Alan, were at an outdoor folk concert in Pennsylvania. During intermission, they headed up a big hill to the restrooms. On her way up the hill, in a sea of people, Barbara saw someone familiar.

She saw Sue.

"We recognized each other at the same time," Barbara says. "I said, 'Wow, what are you doing here? How are you?' She told me about how she was making jewelry, and in a relationship, and just very happy in her life. And I could tell that she was—she looked happier, healthier. She was almost glowing."

They traded a little more small talk, but suddenly Sue grew quiet.

"Barbara," she said, "do you remember the night you gave me that book?"

Barbara gasped.

"I'd forgotten all about it," she says. "When she mentioned it, it hit me like a thunderbolt. It almost knocked me over. She didn't say anything else, and neither did I. I immediately knew why she brought it up. I just grabbed her and hugged her and we both started crying. We hugged and cried for a while."

What went unspoken between them was this: that moment in Pier 1 had been a turning point for Sue.

A *major* turning point.

"Barbara handing me that book was an immensely powerful thing," Sue says now, choking up. "I still get teary talking about it. The book was helpful, but it wasn't about the book. It was about the gesture. Barbara giving me a gift changed my life."

Sue's pain and heartbreak on that night were real—very real. "I was so scared," she remembers. "My whole future was suddenly this frightening reality. When my boyfriend broke up with me, it was like an asteroid hit me and knocked me off course. I was really crashing. And Barbara came in and changed the direction of my life."

Had she really been suicidal that night?

"Who knows?" Sue says. "I certainly thought I was. It was very real to me. Life didn't feel like it was worth living, and no one was taking me seriously. I don't know what I would have done that night."

She never had to find out, because Barbara came back and gave her a book.

"The reason it was such a powerful gift is because it came at just the right moment," says Sue. "To have someone who was basically a stranger do this for me and care about me—it changed the way I felt right on the spot. It made me hopeful for the future. And since that night, I've never felt that bad and that low again. I've never taken anything that seriously again. My whole outlook of the world was suddenly different."

"It was a really simple gesture, but the effect *snowballed*."

Barbara had no idea her little gift meant so much to Sue—until she saw her at the folk concert. The moment had slipped out of her mind, like a thousand other throwaway moments—until Sue mentioned it nine years later.

But the instant she was reminded of it, she knew it had been a turning point.

And in that instant, she discovered her invisible thread.

"I understood that giving Sue the book meant someone cared about her," Barbara says. "At that moment, all she needed was one person to show her they cared. Just one person. Sometimes, that's all it takes."

Barbara and Sue became Facebook friends, and they still exchange messages once in a while. Barbara shares stories of her life—she's a toy sales rep and a yoga teacher—and Sue talks about her husband and her two children and her jewelry business. "We never talk about that night and the book," says Barbara. "We don't need to. It's casual now. I'll send her a note saying, 'Love to the curly-haired Deadhead, hope all is well,' and she'll send back a picture of SpongeBob smiling and kissing."

Yet neither of them has forgotten that long-ago night and likely never will.

"Ever since then, I've realized how extremely blessed I am in my life," Sue says. "Now, I'm always looking for opportunities to do something like that for someone else. It might just be picking up my neighbor's trash when the wind blows it over, that sort of thing. It's just, 'How can I do something nice? How can I pay it forward?'"

Barbara, too, has been changed by their connection. "It made me realize that even a small gesture can be incredibly powerful," she says. "You can do something that almost seems like nothing, but the effect can be profound."

So—what *was* it that made Barbara turn on her heels in that mall? What mysterious force drew her back to Sue?

"It was a tug," she says. "I was being pulled. The feeling was, 'You need to do something *right now*.' The tug was so strong it stopped me in my tracks."

That moment taught Barbara a lesson she has never forgotten.

"What I learned is that we have to heed that tug," she says. "Maybe you will feel it like a pull. Maybe it'll be like a little voice inside you. But whatever it is, we need to tune into it, and we need to *follow it*."

PART FIVE
UNIQUENESS

There are a lot of reasons to think we can't be angels on earth. We don't have any money to donate. We don't have any time to volunteer. We don't have any wisdom to impart, or help to lend, or support to give. "Other people will make better angels than I will," we think. But that's nonsense. As these stories taught me, we are all uniquely suited to be the angels we need to be. Not just a few of us—ALL of us. That's how it works. There is no such thing as an unimportant, uninspiring, unconnected life.

19

THE ADVANCE

Debbie Shore needed an office.

She and her brother, Billy, had an idea—a really *big* idea—to tackle one of the world's most pressing problems. They had a vision, and determination, and optimism—but first, they needed an office. So they asked around and found a landlord who showed them an available room in a building in Washington, D.C.

It was in the basement. It was dark and dusty. It had no furniture. Eerily, every inch of the walls was covered with sound-muffling egg cartons.

Previously, it had been used to treat electroshock therapy patients.

Debbie Shore looked around the spooky room and said three words: "We'll take it."

~≈≥≥≈~

Debbie's story is about big dreams and small first steps.

I crossed paths with Debbie and Billy Shore because their visionary idea involved something I am very interested in: childhood hunger. I have never forgotten what an eleven-year-old Maurice said to me when I saw him on the corner of Broadway thirty years ago—he said, "I am hungry." I later learned he hadn't had anything to eat in two days, and his stomach felt as if he'd been repeatedly punched.

When I looked into it, I discovered that more than 16 *million* children in America face hunger issues. That is one out of every five children! I searched for some way I could contribute to lessening the problem, and that's how I heard about Debbie and Billy.

I learned that Debbie grew up in a small town near Pittsburgh, and she inherited her charitable nature from her parents. Her father, a lawyer and top aide to a congressman, "was a very quiet, content, giving man," Debbie told me. "I don't ever remember him buying anything for himself. He had only one pair of pants and one pair of shoes that I can remember. He lived to serve his family and his community." Most days, Debbie recalls, her father would be on the front porch helping a neighbor with something— an insurance problem, an immigration issue, a school application. "My father took all the calls and handled everything," she says. "He was the go-to guy."

Growing up, Debbie and Billy had been close, but when they hit their teenage years they drifted apart. "We were very different," she says. "Billy was a straight arrow, and I was into alternative music, alternative lifestyles—alternative anything." She studied literature and philosophy at Ohio University, and after college she went to work for a foreign student association. Billy became a legislative assistant for the presidential candidate Gary Hart. One day, he called Debbie to ask if she wanted to volunteer on the campaign. She said yes.

The time they spent working together on the campaign would prove hugely important. In 1984, Billy called Debbie to tell her about an article he'd just read. "It was about the thousands of people who were dying of starvation in Ethiopia, and the millions who were at risk," she says. "Billy said, 'I think I want to start an organization to address this.'"

Imagine that—your brother calls you out of the blue and says he wants to fight famine in Africa. Debbie's reaction was instant. "I told him, 'That sounds great!'" she says. "There was no fear, no doubt, no hesitation. All I remember thinking is, 'It feels right, so let's just go for it.'"

Their initial conversation about starting an organization didn't last very long. "It was about a half a minute," Debbie says. "I was young enough that I felt I could just jump in." Still, how do you conjure an organization to combat hunger out of thin air? What is the first step?

Get an office, of course.

Which led to their first significant hurdle: neither Debbie nor Billy had any money to get things going.

So they took out a two thousand-dollar cash advance on a credit card and rented the electroshock therapy room in the basement.

From the start, they had two essential things going for them—the first was know-how. Their time working with Gary Hart "was the key learning experience for me," Debbie says. "We learned how to organize, inspire, influence, craft a message. And also how to use a little smoke and mirrors."

The other asset was vision.

"You have to know what you want to do," Debbie explains. "If you do, then the first step can be a small step. But unless you know where you are going, you have no chance of getting there."

Early on, their organization didn't even have a name. "We asked people to submit names, and we got Grain of Hope and Wheat of Life, names like that," Debbie says. "It was Billy who came up with our name."

Share Our Strength.

"That is still the core value we live by," says Debbie. "Everyone in the world has a strength they can share in the fight against hunger. The owner of a restaurant, an entertainer, a public relations agent, a politician, a corporate leader, a schoolteacher—everyone. Each of us has his or her own unique strength to share."

Debbie and Billy started by sending out fund-raising letters composed on a primitive typewriter. "In our second year, we finally got a computer," Debbie says (Steve Wozniak, one of the cofounders of Apple, donated a few Macs). One of their earliest moves was persuading well-known chefs to join the fight. A lot of people turned them down, but they kept going.

Then they wrote a letter to Alice Waters, a pioneer in organic, locally grown cuisine. At the time, they didn't realize how important a figure she was in the restaurant world. "We just wrote to her asking for help, and we received a letter back that read, 'Here is $1,000. What else can I do?'" Debbie recalls. "We looked her up and we said, 'Wow, this is a really big deal!'" Once Alice Waters was on board, other top chefs followed.

In its first two years, Share Our Strength didn't raise much money. But eventually, a small food-and-wine tasting they organized raised funds that enabled them to give out their first grant—eight thousand dollars for a food airlift in Ethiopia.

Then Debbie and Billy decided to hone their organization's focus. They realized that hunger wasn't just a problem in Africa—it was a major problem in the United States, too. "It's different, of course," Debbie says, "but hunger exists here."

So Share Our Strength targeted hunger in the United States. The vision grew larger.

More than thirty years later, Share Our Strength and its No Kid Hungry campaign have had a major impact on America's children.

No Kid Hungry is ending childhood hunger in America by connecting children in need to programs that offer school breakfasts and summer meals and by teaching low-income families how to shop for and prepare healthy, affordable foods. Since the campaign's launch, No Kid Hungry and its partners have provided children with more than *460 million meals*. And in just the past two years, it has added nearly one million children to the school breakfast program.

Since their humble beginnings in a basement, Debbie and Billy have raised more than half a billion dollars to combat hunger and poverty. Today, Share Our Strength is renowned for finding scalable, pragmatic solutions to big social problems.

"Our children need to be healthy in order to inherit this country," Debbie says. "There are literally millions of children who aren't healthy. We need to keep pushing to make the national conversation about more than just hunger, but also all the consequences of hunger—the effect it has on our education, health care, national security, and building a competitive workforce."

A good portion of Debbie's time is spent talking to people, looking at programs, and finding out what's broken. For instance, Debbie learned that while 22 million children rely on free and reduced-price meals, only 4 million receive free meals during the summer. "It's not the lack of food or programs or services—it's a lack of access that's the problem," she says. "We have plenty of food for hungry kids, but there are barriers in the way, like stigma, transportation, and red tape."

For instance, Debbie looked into a free summer meal program in New Mexico. The need was there, but participation was low. "We talked to people on the ground, and they said the food was served outdoors, when it was too hot for the children to be outside," Debbie says. "We brought in a big red umbrella, and the children came."

That simple fix was only possible because Share Our Strength went looking for the problem. "You have to see things with your own eyes," she says. "You have to bear witness."

Debbie's work with Share Our Strength was so satisfying and so rewarding, she never thought twice about her chosen career. She also didn't get married, and she had no children. "I just found my niche with Share Our Strength," she says. "I could have taken a different career path, but where else could I have had this kind of impact? Making money does not come close to the ripple effect of what we've done."

Then something remarkable happened.

When Debbie was forty-six, she learned she was pregnant.

"I'd never felt the pressure to be a mother," she says. "I didn't have that ticking biological clock. So when I got pregnant at forty-six, I was kind of distraught. It was the surprise of my life."

Very quickly, a new emotion took hold. "It was like, all of a sudden, the clouds parted," she says. "I thought, 'This is my chance to be a mom!' And the minute Sofia was born, I felt a sense of peace I'd never felt before. It was a blessing beyond anything."

Having a child of her own deepened her feelings about Share Our Strength.

"Now that I was a mother, I realized I was responsible for making sure my daughter was fed and healthy," she said. "She's fourteen now, and I still ask her every day what she's eaten. If I've learned anything in my work—and through my experience as a mom—it's that poverty is complex, but feeding a child is not."

MOVING THE NEEDLE

In 2013, I gave a speech to about two hundred students at a middle school in Ohio. I told them the story of Maurice and me, and I explained my belief that a single act of kindness can make a much bigger difference than we can imagine. I also talked about the importance of appreciating the many blessings we have, especially since so many people aren't as fortunate.

After the speech, I opened the floor to the students so we could all have a conversation about kindness and making a difference. I was encouraged by how enthusiastic and thoughtful the students were. As far as I could tell, they were captivated by the story of Maurice and me, and my message was getting through to them. But the truth is, I can never be sure if it is.

When the Q&A was finished, I was invited to have lunch in the school cafeteria. While I was waiting in line, a cafeteria worker asked me a question: "What happened this morning?" she said.

"What do you mean?"

"The kids," she said. "All the kids are being so nice. They're complimenting us and saying the food tastes great. I never heard so many students say 'please' and 'thank you.' What happened to them?"

I knew exactly what happened to the students.

Kindness happened.

The simple actions of these students—a kind word, a polite response, a little extra enthusiasm about the burgers and fries—confirmed for me that we are capable of fundamentally changing the landscape of our lives.

Sometimes the problems in our lives and in the world seem so daunting, we begin to think there's nothing we can do to make any real difference—but there is always something we can do. It may not be a big thing, and it may not make a huge difference—but each and every one of us is capable of positively impacting the world around us in our own unique way.

We can all move the needle.

Those middle school students in Ohio learned this lesson just by being a little bit nicer.

The next step for them is learning how each of us is uniquely capable of moving the needle off the scale.

20

THE FIVE

R obin Tartarkin had a challenging childhood. When she was
young her mother was diagnosed with cancer, and she spent
the final years of her life in and out of hospitals. Her father, who
owned a meat business, worked from 4:00 a.m. to late in the day
and was rarely around.

"There was no one to drive me to school, so I was truant all the
time," Robin says. "My father just didn't know how to care for me
without my mother around. I was on my own."

No one sat her down and prepared her for what was coming.
No one even spoke to her about her mother's illness. "I would
hear things about how horrible it was for her," she says. "How they
put her in a bed of ice to try to save her life. And then one day my
father just said to me, 'Your mother has cancer, and she will be in
the hospital from now on.'"

Robin remembers visiting her mother toward the end. "She
was so sick, just a skeleton, and I sat there and held her hand for
five minutes," she says. "When I left her room, I said, 'I can't go
back there again.' It was so overwhelming."

Her mother died forty-eight hours later. Robin was just
fourteen.

Robin's father stoically carried on with his life. Meanwhile
Robin failed the eighth grade and lived with continued anxiety.

The ninth grade was just as difficult. Finally, a woman her father was dating suggested he send Robin away to an all-girl boarding school in upstate New York. "I was still grieving for my mother," she says. "I didn't know what to do. So I agreed to go."

Her three years at the boarding school were a brutal experience, and the next few years of her life were a nightmare. She dropped out of college after her first semester and wound up living on the streets. She developed a serious skin disease. More than once, she contemplated suicide. "I was a completely lost soul," she says. "I had no friends, no relatives, no one asking how I was doing. I was totally alone in the world."

There were so few moments of love and kindness in Robin's life that she was able to count them.

"During that part of my journey, there were five people who offered me an act of kindness," she says. "Most of them were really small and simple gestures. Someone said, 'Robin, you're so beautiful.' Someone else said, 'Robin, if only you would smile more.' Two other people showed an interest in me this way. I didn't have anyone in my life who gave me direction of any kind, so these people who offered me encouragement and advice were hugely important."

The fifth kind person changed the course of Robin's life.

She was working in a showroom at a trade center when her boss began to sexually harass her. "He saw how naive and vulnerable I was, and he took advantage of that," Robin remembers. "He was doing it right there in the showroom. But there was another vendor working across the hall who was able to see it happening."

The man pulled Robin aside and said, "I think you need a new job."

He set up an interview for her at a large corporate retail office, and she got the job. "I was twenty-two, and that was a turning point in my life," she says. "I still had issues, but that incident propelled me to believe in myself. That was the beginning of me becoming a stronger person."

Robin can't remember the man's last name or the names of any of the other people who offered her acts of kindness. Those events happened nearly forty years ago. But she has never forgotten the powerful impact those five people had on her life.

"For so many years, it was like I had been buried with my mother," she says. "It was as though I were in the ground with her, and people were peering down at me and saying, 'Let's see you dig your way out of this.' And that's what I did—I dug my way out of that grave. And I couldn't have done it without those five kind people."

Robin went on to get married to a wonderful man and have two beautiful sons. In high school her boys were popular and athletic, and Robin got involved in their schooling. "I was always at PTA meetings and helping with school functions," she says. "For four years I was the chairperson of the high school's Project Graduation, where we had a lockdown party that prevented students from driving drunk on graduation night. I helped raise money, and I had a team of volunteers working with me. In a way, I got to experience high school again vicariously through my sons."

This was when a new set of five people entered—and changed—her life.

One day, Robin's son Jeffrey, who played on the football team, asked her, "Mom, is it okay if some of my teammates come over after the game Friday night?"

Robin told him that was fine.

On Friday night, Jeffrey came home with five teenagers from the team. They were American citizens whose families were from Haiti. They lived in south Florida, but they were bused in to Boca Raton, where Robin lived, to attend Jeffrey's high school. "There was Jason, who was the top athlete on the football team, and also Georry, Daniel, Lorence, and Jean," Robin says. "I didn't know much about them, but they came to our house after every Friday night game. That became our little ritual."

One Friday night, Robin casually asked the boys what their plans were for college. All she got in return were blank stares.

"They were seniors, but they hadn't even taken their SATs yet," she says. "They weren't prepared in any way. When I heard that, I got angry. No one was looking out for these kids, and I knew what that was like."

Then Robin asked the boys, "Okay, which of you *wants* to go to college?"

All five boys raised their hands.

"Right then and there, that became my mission," Robin says. "I was going to give these boys the guidance they needed."

<hr />

Robin was relentless. She signed the five boys up for free ACT and SAT classes. She set up a schedule and picked them up after school so they could prepare their college applications. "I got into trouble with the high school football coach because they were missing practice each week," she says. "The coach would call me and say, 'Where are they?'"

Robin helped the five research colleges, wrangle reference letters, write essays, prepare transcripts, and make football tapes. She gave them a list of colleges and helped them pick the best ones. She took a class on how to file for financial aid and looked into scholarships for the boys. She paid for, prepared, and mailed about five applications for each boy, and she made sure they didn't miss their deadlines.

"My friends would ask me, 'Why are you doing all this?' and I'd say, 'Why not?'" Robin says. "That became my way of looking at life: Don't ask, 'Why?' when you can say, 'Why not?' I adored those boys, and I was going to help them and give them hope, because I could. It was that simple."

But there was something else driving Robin—something deeper.

"When I was their age, I never received that kind of guidance from anyone," she says. "If I had, I think I could have been president of the United States. I feel like I lost so many years of my life when I was all alone and confused. And I couldn't go back and fix that, but I could darn well fix it in the lives of these five kids."

Still, Robin didn't know if her efforts would be in vain. She could only hope the five boys would be accepted somewhere. One day, she was home with Daniel, waiting for a college to send a fax with either an acceptance or a rejection. "It was suspenseful," she says. "We didn't know if he would get in. We just sat there waiting for the fax."

Finally the machine began to whir. Slowly a fax crept out.

Robin grabbed it and read it.

"Daniel," she screamed, "you got in!"

Normally calm and reserved, Daniel erupted in excitement.

In the end, all five boys went to—and graduated from—college. They were good, responsible students, and they worked hard. Jason even went on to play in the National Football League.

And Daniel? "He's so bright," Robin says. "We speak often, and he continues to thank me for my guidance." Daniel is now the Epidemiology and Emergency Preparedness Manager for the Florida Department of Health. He has a master's in Public Health and is currently pursuing his PhD. Daniel is also married and has three beautiful children.

"He is out there helping people and saving lives," Robin says proudly. "That makes me feel good. It makes me feel as if I made a difference."

Another one of the five, Georry, has a BA in Public Health Administration and is a case manager with Big Brothers Big Sisters of Broward County in Florida. When Georry's younger brother Kenny was ready to apply to college, it was Georry who stepped in and helped him—with all the tools he'd learned from Robin. Today, Kenny is finishing medical school, and he will start his residency this fall.

The invisible thread, always rippling outward.

Robin now works as a mentor for at-risk high school girls, helping a group of fifty young women navigate all the problems she had to face alone. "I help them write résumés and dress for interviews," she says. "I talk to them about relationships and encourage them to follow their dreams. I try to bolster their self-esteem and make them feel empowered. In a way, working with these girls means I have come full circle in who I am. I am using my life experiences to make a difference in someone else's life."

Just as important, the connections Robin made with the five teenage boys have helped her repair damage that had gone un-repaired for years.

Becoming an angel on earth finally helped Robin *heal*.

"Those five boys changed my life," she says. "I was the Daughter Who Grew Up Without a Mother. That was my identity. I was the motherless child. Those scars will never go away, but being able to help those boys—being able to offer them kindness and encouragement—gave me a purpose that had been missing in my life. It made me feel that *this is what I was meant to do*. It gave me a new focus and a new identity."

And all that was possible because instead of asking, "Why?" Robin asked, "Why not?"

"All I did was give those boys the motivation, confidence, and attention I'd never had growing up," she says. "It was just being *present* for them. Sometimes, that's all we need to do."

SCAR TISSUE

What I've learned from people like Robin Tartarkin is that it's not just our strengths and triumphs in life that make us uniquely suited to be angels on earth.

It is also our wounds and setbacks.

When I talk about uniqueness, this is what I mean—an understanding that everything that's happened to us, both the good and the bad, prepares us for our unique roles in an interconnected world. Once we accept this, and begin to share our hard-gained wisdom with those around us, great things happen.

Even those who believe they are far too broken or far too damaged to be an angel on earth will soon discover that their wounds and scars and weaknesses are exactly what enable them to be angels on earth.

Sometimes scar tissue is really just a superpower in disguise.

21

THE BABYSITTER

This is how Mary Faulkner's letter to me began: "After spending twenty-three years employed by NYNEX, I took a buyout. Then I left my husband of seventeen years, put my house on the market, and took a job at one-third my former salary. Finally, I took my fourteen-year-old son, rented a house, and got my Realtor's license. I had no idea what would happen next."

Basically, Mary Faulkner started over. She took a deep breath and tried for a new beginning. Reading her note, I marveled at the courage it must have taken for her to upend her life so thoroughly. "Yes, it was frightening," Mary would later say. "I was miserable and I knew I needed to start over, but it was scary. I was terrified of making the wrong decision."

What helped her push through the fears and doubts, what kept her going through all the uncertainty, was something her grandmother had told her years and years ago. "My grandmother had a strong Catholic faith, and when I was growing up she had a big impact on me," says Mary. "And what she told me was something I never, ever forgot. It was so simple. She said, 'Mary, God sends you where you are supposed to be.'"

Mary was at her new job in a small real estate firm on New York's Long Island when a young woman in her twenties, Carissa, walked into the office. Carissa was carrying a four-month-old baby boy in a car seat. She asked Mary to help her find a house to rent in town. As an afterthought, she also asked Mary if she could recommend a nanny.

"I don't know any nannies," Mary said, "but if you get stuck and need a babysitter, give me a call."

To this day, Mary isn't sure why she said that. "I guess I thought, 'She doesn't know anyone here, and she has this young child; it's the decent thing to do,'" Mary says. "But babysitting wasn't anything I ever planned to do."

Two weeks later, though, Carissa called Mary at 8:00 p.m. "She said she had to go into the city for some kind of photo shoot," Mary recalls, "and she asked if I could come over and watch her son." Mary was skeptical—what kind of photo shoot happens late at night and at the last minute? Even so, she agreed to help.

Mary drove to the condo she'd found for Carissa, a mile from where she lived. The infant—Santino—was already asleep in his crib. Mary stayed with the boy that evening—and, as it turned out, the whole night. Carissa didn't get home until 6:00 a.m.

"I thought it would be a couple of hours," Mary says. "Something was fishy, but I didn't think it was my business to ask. Then Carissa handed me one hundred dollars, which I really needed at the time. I told her if she ever got stuck again, she should call me."

And so Mary became Santino's babysitter. The calls became more frequent, the excuses stranger. "She'd say the parking garage was closed and she couldn't get her car until the next morning and ask if I could spend the night watching Santino," Mary says.

"Then it became, 'I have to go to Florida for the weekend.' I knew I didn't approve of whatever it was she was doing, but I also knew that her son would be safe with me."

Eventually, Mary bought a baby car seat, a portable playpen, and a whole bunch of toys. She began bringing Santino back to her home so she could watch him there. Mary introduced Santino to Thomas the Tank Engine, who quickly became his favorite toy. Mary also toilet trained the little boy. "He had no other relatives come see him, ever," says Mary of Santino, whose family lived in the Northwest. "Basically, he was like my kid. He called me Mimi."

Still, he had a mother, and Mary was careful not to overstep her bounds. She told herself that getting too close to Santino was a bad idea. Once, Carissa sent Santino to visit an aunt in Arizona for two weeks and asked Mary to drop him off and pick him up at the airport. "I was at JFK waiting for Santino to come back, and all of a sudden I saw him and his aunt coming down the hallway, and I yelled out, 'Santino!'" Mary says. "And when he saw me, he ran down the hall and jumped in my arms and cupped my face with his little hands and hugged me as hard as he could. That was the moment. That was the point of no return for me. I knew he already had a mother. But I was his mother, too."

As time passed, Mary grew more and more frustrated with Carissa. When Carissa asked her to watch Santino on Mother's Day, Mary told her, "I have plans, and it would be nice if you could come home and spend some time with your son." Carissa agreed to return home to be with Santino, but she never showed up. "I just couldn't understand why she didn't care more about her son," Mary says. "I couldn't fix the situation, but I could feel myself becoming more and more emotionally involved in it. There was nothing I could do."

It was around then that Carissa began to resent how close Mary and Santino were getting. One day, when Santino was four, Carissa announced that she and her son were moving to Hawaii. "So that's that," Mary thought. "I will miss him, but this is how it has to be." She babysat for him one last time and sadly waved goodbye as Carissa whisked him away. "Then he was gone," Mary says. "It was heartbreaking."

Mary's grandmother had been right: she wound up precisely where she needed to be. Not just for herself, but for Santino, a special boy who came out of nowhere, graced her life for a little while, and then disappeared. Perhaps he'd only needed her for the few years they were together. If that was the case, then at least she'd been there for him, and kept him safe, and tried to make him happy.

"We just got pulled apart, that's all," Mary says.

But then, six months after Carissa and Santino moved away, Mary got a call from a social worker in Hawaii.

"Carissa has been arrested," he told her. "Santino is in emergency foster care."

Carissa had had some kind of breakdown. She'd been taken to jail and refused to give police or social workers any information about Santino. Authorities also questioned a friend of hers, who told them what they needed to do. "Call Mary Faulkner," the friend said. "She knows everything."

Mary spent hours on the phone with Santino's caseworkers, sharing everything she knew about him and his medical history. "When he'd had his vaccines, his pediatrician's number, all of that," she says. "They were amazed at how I knew it all." One social worker told her Santino could really use a visit from someone he knew and trusted. "Can you possibly come to Hawaii to see him?" he asked.

Of course, Mary wanted to go—but she couldn't. "I was a single mother, and I just couldn't afford it," she says. "How could I ever afford Hawaii?"

Santino, it seemed, would just have to get through his nightmare alone.

Then something remarkable happened.

In the four years that Mary had spent caring for Santino, she had introduced him to many of her friends and colleagues and relatives. They all knew his story, and they all knew Mary's story, too. When they learned what was happening in Hawaii, they sprang into action.

"First my aunt and uncle called and said they were giving me their frequent-flier miles for the plane ticket," Mary says. "Then one of my clients gave me his points for a rental car. And then a builder gave me his time-share in Hawaii for two weeks. They all came together just to help Santino, and before I knew it, I was on a plane to Hawaii."

When Santino saw Mary, he burst into tears and hugged her and didn't let go. "The time-share was a two-bedroom condo, and he stayed with me there," Mary says. "One night, he came up to me crying and said, 'Please don't make me go back to the vegetable house.' His emergency foster parents were native Hawaiians, and I guess they ate a lot of fish and vegetables. I wanted to tell Santino everything would be okay, but I couldn't. I didn't want to make any promises I couldn't keep."

LAURA SCHROFF

Eventually, the state of Hawaii granted temporary custody of Santino to his aunt. "The social worker told me, 'We always find in favor of a blood relative,'" Mary says. "And then he said, 'Thanks for your help, but we don't need you anymore.'"

Mary was devastated but did her best to move on. From time to time she sent little packages to Santino—toy trains and other things she knew he liked. But otherwise, she resigned herself to the sad reality: she and Santino had been pulled apart yet again.

But then . . .

Almost a year later, Mary's cell phone lit up with an incoming call. She was in a Chinese restaurant, in the middle of a negotiation for a mortgage with a Chinese buyer. "It was a four-way conversation with me and the buyer and the mortgage broker and a Chinese interpreter, and all of a sudden I got this call," Mary says. "I really didn't have time to take it, but something told me I needed to."

Mary took the call and heard the voice of Santino's aunt.

"We can't do this anymore," the aunt said. "I'm putting Santino in foster care."

It was happening again. Santino was being dragged into the system again. He was being packed off to live with strangers again. If the boy's aunt had already notified social services and started the paperwork, there was nothing Mary could do. He would be plunged back into his nightmare yet again.

In fact, Santino's aunt *had* called social services.

But it happened to be a legal holiday, so no one answered.

"That was divine intervention," Mary says. "I immediately called my lawyer to see what I could do to get Santino."

Then Mary called her own son, George. For a long time, it had been just the two of them, and Mary wanted to be sure her son was okay with her trying to bring Santino home.

"His aunt doesn't want him anymore," she told him.

"Well," George said, "we do."

"It was a very short conversation," Mary says now. "I told George I loved him and got off the phone and went to get Santino."

Mary filed the paperwork to become Santino's temporary guardian. When she went to pick him up—"Rescue Day, we called it"—all of his belongings were in a big pile on his aunt's front porch. As Mary drove away with him, she looked through their kitchen window and noticed his aunt and her husband giving each other a high five.

Back at her home, Mary began the process of trying to adopt Santino. Meanwhile, an official notified her that Carissa had been released from prison and was back on Long Island. Mary was worried she might show up at their home or at Santino's school, so she alerted school officials and had a candid talk with Santino about his mother. "He was so scared after that," Mary says. "He said, 'What if she comes to take me?' I told him we would never let that happen. He said, 'What if she breaks the basement window in the middle of the night and takes me?' I said, 'Santino, it's okay. You're not going anywhere.'"

One morning, he woke up crying.

"What's wrong?" Mary asked.

"I can't remember her face," Santino said. "I can't remember my mother's face."

"Okay," Mary said. "Just go in the bathroom and look in the mirror."

Santino hopped out of bed and did just that.

"That's her face, right there," Mary told him.

Then she asked if he missed his mother.

"Sometimes," he said.

"Why don't you ever tell me you feel that way?"

"I don't want to make you feel bad," Santino answered.

Mary pulled him tight and assured him he could never, ever make her feel bad for loving his mother.

"Think of it this way," she told him. "You have two mothers."

The process of legally gaining custody of Santino took years. For a while, it looked as if it might not happen. Mary was Santino's temporary guardian, but his aunt was still his legal guardian, and his future was in her hands. Whatever she decided to do, that would be it. For months, his aunt refused to sign papers relinquishing custody to Mary. Social workers in Hawaii told Mary there was nothing more they could do. "It was painful," says Mary, "but even then my thought was, 'Okay, Santino's with me now, and I'm not letting him go.'"

Finally, Santino's aunt relinquished custody to Mary. "Santino was in kindergarten when we started it and in the second grade when we finished," Mary says. "His adoption became official on January 24, but we never celebrated that day. The truth is, he was part of our family already."

A few years after the adoption, Mary learned that Carissa had passed away. She sat Santino down to break the sad news to him.

"Your mother has gone to heaven," she told him. "She always loved you very much; she just wasn't able to take care of you, or herself."

Santino listened and nodded, but he didn't cry. That summer, he joined some of his relatives in Montana, so he could be there when they sprinkled his mother's ashes from high up on a mountaintop.

Today, Santino is eighteen and headed to college. He is smart and has a dry sense of humor, and he is shooting for a career designing computer games. "He's like any teenager; we have our ups and downs," Mary says. "But he is such a wonderful kid, and I have the highest hopes for him."

Together they have already beaten the odds, just by remaining in each other's lives. "I really thought I'd lost him a few times," Mary says. "I can't even explain how this all happened. Maybe it's not even explainable. So many things had to happen a certain way. I had to decide to start my life over, I had to go to work in that real estate office, his aunt had to decide to give him up on a legal holiday—all of this stuff had to come together in just the perfect way. And it did."

When I heard Mary's remarkable story, I understood what that "unexplainable" thing really was. It was an invisible thread.

"Santino and I kept getting pulled apart," Mary says. "But we kept finding each other, too."

TWO-WAY STREETS

I never wanted anyone to think that I was Maurice's savior, that I swooped in to rescue him from whatever fate awaited him on the streets. That is far too simplistic a description of what really happened. Maurice had a mother, and he had a family. And though his mother was addicted to drugs and unable to care for him, I knew he loved his mother very much, and I never wanted him to stop loving her. All I did was try to let Maurice be a kid for a while.

I tried to let him know that someone cared about him.

In fact, Maurice and I made a kind of bargain.

The first time I cooked dinner for him in my apartment, he was clearly nervous. He didn't know what I wanted from him, and his life on the streets had taught him to be cautious. I didn't know it at the time, but Maurice came to my apartment with a box cutter in his pocket, just in case.

Before dinner, I told Maurice I had something very important to say.

"The reason I invited you to my apartment is because I consider you my friend," I said. "Friendship is built on trust, and I want you to know I will never betray that trust. I want you to know you will always be able to trust me. But if you betray my trust, we can no longer be friends. Do you understand?"

I wanted Maurice to be aware that our friendship was a two-way street. But when I finished, he looked at me with his big eyes and seemed confused.

"Is that it?" he finally asked. "You just want to be my friend?"

"Yes, that's it," I said.

Maurice relaxed and let down his guard. Then he stood up and put out his hand. I put my hand out, and we shook hands.

"A deal's a deal," Maurice said.

And so we made our special bargain. We didn't want anything from each other, except to be friends.

So far, that bargain has lasted thirty years.

What I've learned over the last five years is that when we decide to honor our invisible thread connections and try to play a positive role in someone's life, we are not entering into a one-way bargain—we help, they get helped. There is no such thing as a one-way angel on earth. If anything, the bargain is lopsided in our favor.

Because the dynamic of any invisible thread connection is that the blessings always flow both ways.

_____

22

THE BARGAIN

Deb Howe Allen was in her Honda sedan, on her way to the local community college, when it happened—a panic attack.

She knew she would be nervous, but she didn't think it would be this bad. After all, it had been her decision—no one pushed her into it. And what was there to be so nervous about? No matter how it went, it would all be over in two short weeks.

Still—Deb Allen panicked.

She was going to host a child sponsored by the Fresh Air Fund.

The Fresh Air Fund has been around since 1877, providing free, two-week vacations for underprivileged children ages six to twelve. Deb had grown up surrounded by children. She had only one brother, but she also had nine uncles, ten aunts, and twenty-eight cousins. "Half of our childhood was spent around extended family," she says.

After college, she was single and living in a house she'd just purchased in Rochester, New York. That's when she made the decision that led to her panic attack. She got the idea from her best friend's mother, and she liked it so much she decided to try it herself.

"My house was small, but I did have an extra bedroom, and I didn't have children of my own," Deb says. "I called someone at the Fresh Air Fund and asked if they allowed single people to play host, and they said, 'Sure.' Then they asked me if I preferred a girl or a boy, and I said a girl."

And that was that: Deb was about to become a volunteer host.

There was only one problem—she didn't think she could do it.

For one thing, she didn't have an extra bed in her new home, or a lot of furniture. Nor did Deb have any experience caring for children. Overall, she felt completely unequipped to give the child a memorable experience. The only good thing was that she was hosting a girl. She might instinctively know how to handle a girl.

Then, two days before the beginning of her adventure, Deb received a call from a Fresh Air Fund staffer.

"We have a six-year-old boy we are trying to place," the staffer said. "Can you take him instead?"

"I thought, 'Well, I can't really say no,'" Deb remembers, "so I said okay."

Two days later, she was in her old Honda sedan, on the way to the local community college, where a bus would drop off the boy.

That's when she had her panic attack.

"I thought, 'What on earth are you doing? How are you possibly going to keep this boy busy for two weeks? What if he hates you?' I was way, way out of my comfort zone."

She parked her car and watched a bus pull into the lot. One by one, children stepped out and were greeted by couples and families. Then a little boy came down and saw a single, nervous woman waiting for him.

"Hi, I'm Deb," she said to him.

"Hi," the boy said with a beaming smile. "I'm Solomon."

Solomon lived in the Bronx with his mother and three siblings. At six, he was the oldest child. Because his father wasn't around,

Solomon had to play a big role in helping raise the other children. "He was like a surrogate parent," Deb says. "When you are as young as he was, that's a lot of work. He couldn't just be a kid."

On their first day together, Deb took Solomon to the supermarket so they could stock up on foods he liked. He asked for Pop-Tarts and Hamburger Helper. That evening, they sat down for dinner, and afterward Solomon made an announcement: "I like everything you make!" he said.

Deb felt proud of herself—she'd prepared a meal he enjoyed.

Then Solomon said, "My mother told me I have to eat everything you make."

"That's when I stopped patting myself on the back," Deb says.

Deb also found a way to make her new home more hospitable for Solomon. Just days before his arrival, Deb borrowed a bed and a rug from a friend and found a lamp and a nightstand at the Salvation Army. The room was perfectly cozy for Solomon on his first night.

Yet he barely slept.

It was the first time he'd ever had a bedroom all to himself.

On the second night, Solomon walked into Deb's room in the middle of the night, disoriented.

"What's wrong?" Deb asked.

"It feels weird," Solomon said. "It's too quiet."

Deb sat with him in his bedroom until he finally fell asleep.

Solomon didn't talk very much about his family. But Deb was able to catch glimpses of what his life was probably like in the Bronx. One day he asked her, "Does anyone in your neighborhood have guns? Do you feel safe here?" Another time, as he walked up the stairs to the second floor, he saw Deb's car parked in the driveway. "Your car's still there!" he yelled out.

"That showed me what he was dealing with," says Deb. "He was seeing stuff at home that most kids don't have to deal with."

Day by day, the trust between them built, and their friendship grew. One afternoon, Deb was driving home with Solomon when she spotted a roadside fruit stand. She pulled over and pointed to a little box of raspberries.

"Do you like these?" she asked Solomon.

"I think so."

Deb bought a box and asked Solomon to hold it. By the time they got home, the box was completely empty.

"I guess you like raspberries," Deb said.

"Yes," said Solomon, "I guess I do."

The two weeks passed quickly. Solomon's cheerful, positive nature endeared him to all of Deb's friends, and to her. She took him swimming in her friends' pools, and she took him to the Seabreeze Amusement Park, where he rode a famous roller coaster called the Jackrabbit. They also went to flea markets and garage sales.

"He really liked helping me find deals," Deb says. "That became our sort of shared favorite word—'bargain.' We were out there hunting bargains together."

Deb knew that Solomon's seventh birthday fell not long after his last day with her. So she threw him an early party—cake, ice cream, and games in the backyard. She bought him a present—a soccer ball—and she watched him happily run around in the grass with her friends' children. Before she knew it, she was driving Solomon back to the community college, where he got back on the bus and went home.

"I was happy I did it, but I said to myself, 'Well, I won't do *that* again,'" Deb says. "It was just too exhausting."

The next spring, Deb's friends began asking if she'd be hosting Solomon again. They asked because they wanted to see him. Deb realized she missed him, too. "I was like a mother who forgets the labor pains and says, 'Yeah, I can do this again,'" she recalls. "And if I was going to do it, I wanted to do it with Solomon."

That summer, she drove to meet the bus and pick up her little friend again. The summer after that, she did it again. And the summer after that, and the next one, too.

In all, Deb and Solomon spent six wonderful summers together, until Solomon turned twelve and was too old to stay in the program.

The last day of their last summer, Deb threw him another birthday party. This time, she gave him a special present. "He loved whales and dolphins," she says, "so I made him a quilt with all these bright blues and greens and whales and dolphins." It was difficult for them to say goodbye, but they promised to stay friends.

But then Solomon became a teenager, and "we began to lose touch," Deb says. "I didn't hear from his family a lot. Then a whole year went by without any word, and I tried to call him. But their phone had been disconnected."

⁓⟫⟪⁓

Several years passed. Deb had no idea what was happening with Solomon. She was worried he was having a hard time. She was afraid he'd lost his way.

Then, out of the blue, Solomon called.

It was as if no time had passed at all. "He came back up to see me that summer," Deb says. "I was dating Jim, who became my husband, and we all hung out together." Not too long after they reconnected, Deb began planning her wedding, and she knew one guest she absolutely wanted to be there.

"I called Solomon's mother, and I told her I wanted him at the wedding, and I asked her if it would be okay if I paid for him to fly to Rochester," Deb says. "And she was so excited, she let out a holler. She said, 'Of course! Of course it's okay!'"

But Solomon wasn't just a guest at the wedding.

Deb's father had passed away. Her one sibling, her older brother, couldn't make it to the wedding. That left various uncles and friends who could walk Deb down the aisle. But that's not what Deb wanted.

"I wanted Solomon to do it," she says.

The ceremony was held in an historic cobblestone church in Childs, New York. Deb stood at the back of the church in her flowing white dress. Solomon was there in a dark suit and tie. When the music started, they interlocked arms and walked slowly down the aisle.

"Solomon brought me up to Jim, shook his hand, and gave me a little kiss," Deb says. "It was very sweet."

Deb wanted Solomon to take the walk with her because she felt it was symbolic. "This was me moving from one part of my life to another," she says, "and I needed Solomon to know he'd be part of that new life."

Solomon is thirty-one now, and taking online classes at the University of Phoenix while working four part-time jobs. He has studied psychology, worked in hospitals and group homes, and would like to have a career in counseling. One recent spring, Deb, Jim, and their two children went on vacation to the Grand Canyon, and Solomon met them there. "He stayed with us for a few days, and it was so exciting," she says. "I was so happy we got to see it together."

There are times when Solomon hits a rough patch and emails Deb for a pep talk. "I tell him, 'I admire you so much, keep going, don't give up,'" Deb says. "I hope that hearing that helps him. Knowing someone cares about him is important."

Yet there are also times when it's Deb who needs the pep talk. When she went through a period of unemployment, "Solomon, bless his heart, was so helpful," she says. "I'd email him about all these jobs I didn't get, and he'd write back, 'I can't believe those people didn't hire you! It's their loss, they are missing out. Don't ever give up.'"

Put simply, Deb and Solomon are always there for each other.

"Sometimes, when I talk about Solomon, I will hear comments like, 'Oh, the suburban white lady swoops in to rescue a child,'" Deb says. "*But Solomon didn't need to be rescued.* He had a mother and a family and a life. He just didn't grow up the way I did, and he didn't have the opportunity to ride bikes and do things like that. And that's what I was able to do for him—I helped him enjoy his summer."

In fact, Deb has always thought that, in some ways, Solomon rescued her. It was as if they'd struck a private bargain to be there for each other, somewhere between the box of raspberries and the walk down the aisle.

"What was I to Solomon?" Deb says. "A big sister? A surrogate mother? Just someone in his life? I don't know. Maybe it doesn't even need a name. Let's just say we are very good friends."

Then Deb thought about it a little more.

"I will always have Solomon in my life," she says. "He is better at staying in touch with me than some friends who live ten minutes away. He is a faithful friend, but he is more than that. He is the most faithful friend I have."

PART SIX
CLEARNESS

The stories that follow share a common theme: vision. Not just eyesight or observation, but rather the ability to see things others might not. The ability to look past distractions, preconceptions, and easy conclusions in order to see what's really there. The ability to see with clearness. I call it angel vision: the capacity to notice the angel in everyone. When we learn to trust this vision, we clear the way for miracles to happen.

THE FACILITATOR

Johnny was the kind of student you could look at one of two ways. Either you could see him the way most people saw him— as a really bad student who didn't show much aptitude for anything.

Or you could see him the way his teacher Andy Smallman saw him.

"Reading and writing were difficult for Johnny because he had a learning disability," Andy says of his onetime student in a private elementary school on the west coast. "But he was one of the sweetest, most sincere human beings I've ever met. I was worried he'd end up in a school where someone would tell him there's something wrong with him. But there was nothing wrong with him."

One day, Johnny walked up to Andy with a question.

"Why aren't the newspapers telling us about all the good stuff that's happening?" Johnny wondered. "Because there are way more good things than bad things that happen."

Andy decided to help Johnny create a little pamphlet called *The Good News Newspaper*. "He'd talk to people about any good things they were doing," Andy says. "He didn't want to write about the two cars that got into accidents; he wanted to write about all the cars that made it home safely. He wanted to focus on the positive."

Together, Johnny and Andy accomplished something small but meaningful. But *The Good News Newspaper* was only the start of their story.

~⟋⟍~

Over the last five years, I've shared the story of Maurice and me with thousands of students, from grade school on up to college. I've seen how receptive students are to the themes of kindness and compassion.

All of which has made me wonder: Shouldn't we be teaching kindness in schools?

After all, we teach math and science and physics and literature, because all of these subjects are enriching for our children. But what is more enriching than kindness? Why can't we start teaching kindness in elementary school? Why don't we have a class called Kindness 101?

Is it possible to teach kids kindness just like we teach them algebra?

I began to look into this idea, which is how I came across a dreamer named Andy Smallman.

~⟍⟋~

Andy has been an educator for more than twenty years now, but he doesn't actually refer to what he does as teaching. He calls it facilitating.

Andy started one of the very first, if not *the* first, kindness classes for students. Yet his goal isn't to teach kindness—it's to create an environment in which kindness can flourish.

His philosophy is based on his belief that "we, as human beings, are fundamentally kind." He says, "It's just that a lot of things end up interfering with that along the way."

Andy was born in Omaha, Nebraska; his family moved to Seattle when he was ten. His father was a traveling candy salesman, and his mother was very involved with their community. "She was co-president of the PTA and always volunteering," Andy says. "My parents were the people who, if someone needed a meal, they would prepare it and deliver it."

Andy's own experience in school made him question traditional education. "I felt like my high school wasn't helping me know who I was; it was telling me what I should do," he says. "It gave me grades, but it didn't give me insight into who I was."

Starting in his senior year, Andy worked a string of odd jobs—night manager of a bookstore, DJ in a small town in Alaska, statistician for the *Daily Racing Form*—before a girlfriend steered him toward the Big Brothers Big Sisters program. "I was matched up with a third-grade boy whose father wasn't around," he remembers, "and that's when I realized I was supposed to work with kids. It was like a light shined down on me."

He enrolled at The Evergreen State College, an experimental, nontraditional college an hour south of Seattle. He finished in less than three years, went to graduate school, and earned his teaching certificate.

Then he decided he didn't want to teach.

"From what I could see, teaching was just managing the behavior of kids who were kept in classrooms instead of being allowed to go out and engage authentically with the world," he says. "I started fantasizing about what a twenty-first-century school would look like."

The fantasy became a reality in 1994, when Andy and his wife, Melinda Shaw, founded the Puget Sound Community School in

Seattle. "There were no academic requirements to get in, no test scores, and no grades," Andy says. "We were looking for kids who had a spark and who would naturally challenge themselves."

Ten families signed up to send their children there, and the school was incorporated as a nonprofit. But there was no actual school building, at least not at first. The concept was to make use of donated space and at the same time expose students to real-world situations. Classes were held in conference rooms, churches, and retirement homes. One of Andy's first kindness experiments took place with residents of a retirement home.

"We put our twelve-year-olds together with their eighty-year-olds, and we had them do random acts of kindness," Andy says. In one experiment, Andy and a team of eight—four teenagers, four elders—went to a Starbucks and handed a barista money to cover the bill of the next customer. They secretly watched as a woman came up to pay for her coffee.

As instructed, the barista said, "You have been the victim of a random act of kindness."

For a moment the customer was baffled. But then she smiled warmly and left. Andy and his team "exploded with happiness," he later wrote. "We walked out united in what felt to us like an act of superhero proportions. The elders seemed younger, and the teens wiser."

On another outing, "A local florist gave us some flowers, and we walked around and handed them to some of the senior citizens," Andy recalls. When they gave flowers to one older man, he, too, seemed puzzled, but only for a moment. He told Andy and the students it was the first time anyone had ever given him flowers in his life.

Then he started to cry.

"For our kids to experience that," Andy says, "was amazing."

Yet Andy had even bigger plans to facilitate kindness around the globe. And a lot of the inspiration for that came from one of the first eleven students in his new school.

A student named Johnny.

<hr />

Andy brought Johnny with him from the private school where he'd taught before starting Puget Sound. His worst fear for Johnny—that he would end up in a school where teachers told him something was wrong with him—never came to pass. Instead, Johnny wound up in a school where original thinking was encouraged.

Andy was one of the very first educators in the country to use email as a teaching tool. "This was back in 1994, and schools were afraid of working on the internet," he says. "But I got some dial-up accounts that we could use, and we found a man in Europe who was letting people ask him questions about the Holocaust. We sent out questions and received responses, and I could see how these threads between all these people could potentially cover the earth in goodness."

Andy developed a unique and celebrated class called the Practice of Kindness. Using a small global mailing list, he invited people to participate in a ten-week, back-and-forth discussion about kindness. Each week, the challenge nudged participants further out of their comfort zones. They'd be asked to do something kind for an acquaintance, then for a stranger, then for someone they were in conflict with. "By the tenth week," Andy says, "there was an awareness that doing something kind for yourself *includes* being kind to others."

The Practice of Kindness earned Andy attention from the media and other educators. He began getting calls from teachers wondering how they could introduce kindness into their curriculums. "I always tell them, 'Don't start by talking about kindness; start with appreciation and gratitude,'" he says. "Once kids begin to recognize the good things that are happening all around them, their eyes are opened to all the opportunities the universe gives us to be kind."

Andy's theories about facilitating kindness may not be mainstream educational thinking, but they did pay off for one of his original eleven students—his friend Johnny.

The boy who struggled to read and write now has a graduate degree. "He works with kids on the autism spectrum and helps families with special needs children," Andy says proudly. "I still bring him into the school to talk, and we both tell kindness stories: kind things we did, kind deeds we read about. It's like we're kindness counselors."

It's true that in their time together, Andy taught Johnny quite a bit.

But Johnny also taught Andy life lessons he still relies on today.

"I saw how Johnny and the other students took to the idea of doing kind things right away," he says. "It helped me realize that kindness is inherent to being human. And the younger the children, the easier it is for them to tap into their inherent kindness."

WHAT ARE YOU, CRAZY?

Who writes stories about cars that don't crash?

Who starts a school that has no teachers or tests?

People who see things others don't see, that's who.

The benefits of living with clearness can be astounding, but sometimes there is a cost, too—people might think you're not thinking clearly.

The day I met Maurice, I initially walked right past him. Then I stopped in my tracks in the middle of Broadway—only one of the busiest avenues in the world. The traffic light turned red, and all the cars started honking at me. One cabbie yelled, "What are you, crazy?" Even Maurice remembers seeing me in the middle of the avenue and thinking I was out of my mind.

To anyone who was there, I looked like a woman with her head in the clouds.

But actually, I was experiencing a moment of great clearness.

Because in the next instant, I turned around and went back to Maurice, and my life was forever changed.

And then, for many months afterward, there were people who thought I was making a mistake by having Maurice in my life. They were worried about my safety, and they thought I was putting myself in danger. They wondered if I was making a bad decision.

In fact, it was the best decision I ever made.

To be an angel on earth, you can't be afraid to look silly or crazy or wrong. You can't worry about what other people think. Let the cars honk and the cabbies yell.

Then set forth on your own clear and purposeful path.

THE PURPOSE

Genevieve Piturro was always the determined type. Growing up in Yonkers, New York, she'd get picked up from school by her mother, who one day showed up with a really big umbrella. "I was embarrassed by it, and I insisted she walk behind me," Genevieve remembers with a laugh. "I was insistent. I said, 'Mom, don't walk with me!'"

As she got older, her life plan fell neatly into place. "I wanted to be a single girl living in Manhattan with a dream job and an apartment and everything," she says. "I wanted to be Mary Tyler Moore." After college, she moved out, and her parents didn't speak to her for six months. "Back then it was unheard of for a daughter to leave home," she says. "But they eventually accepted it, and when I bought my own apartment in Riverdale, they couldn't have been more proud of me."

Everything went according to plan: Genevieve climbed the corporate ladder and became a successful public relations and marketing executive. Along the way she had boyfriends who wanted to get married and have children, but "that just wasn't for me," she says. "I didn't have a ticking clock. I always thought there was another path for me." Genevieve did love children, though, and she loved spending time with her sister's kids. She also gave ten percent of her salary to a charity called

Starlight, which granted wishes and gave gifts to hospitalized children.

It was as if the universe had given Genevieve everything she asked for. She was, in every way, living her dream.

Except, she felt that she wasn't.

Genevieve was thirty-eight years old when, out of the blue, on a random day, she felt the need to press pause on her life. "I just stopped what I was doing and I asked myself, 'Is this enough? Am I on the right path? Is this what I should be doing?'" she recalls. "I hadn't asked those questions before, and I don't know why I did that day."

What truly shocked her, however, was the answer that came back from the universe.

"It was very, very clear," she says. "And the response was, 'Maybe not. You might have missed something.'"

<hr>

For the first time, Genevieve began to question her master plan. "I kept asking myself these deep questions," she says. "'Do our lives have a purpose? Do they need to have a purpose? What is my life's purpose?'" She confided to her boyfriend, Demo—who would soon become her husband—about her struggles, and he calmly advised her to keep questioning. "He said, 'Yes, you have a purpose, and you have to figure it out. You really need to think about it. Ask the universe for help.' I didn't know what that meant. He told me to meditate, and I started doing it every day."

And that is when an idea, fully formed, came out of nowhere.

"I decided that what I would do was read to homeless children," Genevieve says. "I always loved children, and I loved reading, and it just made sense. I made some calls and found a homeless shelter where I could come in and read to the kids."

She bought some books and went to some of the worst neighbor-hoods in New York and sat down on the floor with the children and read. "Many of them were separated from their mothers be-cause of drug or police issues, and they were sent to these emer-gency shelters, and I would get a call from a social worker and show up and read with them at night," she says. But one night, after finishing a book, Genevieve stayed around and followed the shelter staffers as they were putting the children to sleep.

What she saw changed her life.

"They brought the kids into this bare room with cots on the floor and a couple of couches, and someone said, 'Okay, time to sleep,' and they turned the lights out, and that was it," she says. "They didn't even have pajamas; they just slept in their street clothes. It was so cold, so awful. The staffers were doing the best they could, and they were being nice, but that was all they were able to do. When I left, I could hear some of the children crying."

Genevieve flashed back to her own childhood. One of her very fondest memories was of her mother coming into her bedroom at night to read to her and tuck her in. "She made up these funny stories about a chocolate bar and peanuts that came to life," she remembers. "And I would make excuses and try to stay awake and say I had to go to the bathroom, just to stretch it out. It was such a warm and loving time, and since then I have heard a million stories about children bonding with their parents at bedtime."

As she was leaving the shelter that night, Genevieve heard herself asking one of the staffers a question. "I didn't even think about it," she says. "I just asked, 'Next time, can I bring pajamas?' And the staffer said, "Of course, what a nice idea.'"

Genevieve went out and bought thirty pairs of new pajamas. "I wanted to make sure there would be enough for all the children who might be there," she says. She went to the shelter and read to the children, same as always, but when she was done reading she said, "Everyone, get in line. I have a surprise for you.'"

The children lined up, and Genevieve handed each one new pajamas. Spiderman pajamas. Cinderella pajamas. Beautiful, colorful, new pajamas. "They were all so excited and so happy," she says. "All of them except one little girl."

When Genevieve handed that girl pajamas, the girl shook her head and said, "No." A bit later Genevieve tried again, but again the girl shook her head. Finally, when all the other children had their pajamas, the little girl came up to Genevieve, who bent down so she could hear the girl's whispered question. "What are these?" the girl asked.

"I just lost it," Genevieve says. "I was a mess. But I tried not to cry in front of the children. I explained to her what pajamas were, and she told me she always wore her pants to bed. So I helped her put them on, and she looked at them and touched them and gave me a huge smile."

Not much later, Genevieve was riding on a subway when a phrase appeared in her head. "Like a raindrop literally plopped into my brain," she says. "It was two words: Pajama Program."

———— ❦ ————

Right there in the crowded subway car, Genevieve said the words aloud: "Pajama Program."

They sounded good. They sounded right. She got off at the next stop and called Demo on a pay phone and told him about her "raindrop" moment.

"Do you know what to do with that idea?" he asked her.

"Yes, I do," she said.

"Then do it."

For the next few weeks, Genevieve could barely eat or sleep.

"I was *so* fired up," she says. "All I could think about were children and pajamas. My mother loved the idea and jumped right on board. She said, 'Follow your heart.' But a lot of other people just thought I was crazy. They said, 'What are you doing? Why are you doing this?' And I'd say, 'I'm trying to find a way to make this my life's purpose.'"

The Pajama Program started small. Genevieve kept buying new pajamas to go along with some donated pajamas she received. Then she got a call from *Parenting* magazine. The editors had heard about her and wanted to run a little story about her program. Genevieve gave the interview and went on with her life.

One afternoon, she returned to her apartment building in Riverdale. "I walked into the lobby, and there were hundreds and hundreds of boxes stacked everywhere," she says. "You couldn't even move. All these tenants were angry and yelling, and I had no idea what was going on."

Then Genevieve realized the tenants were yelling at *her*.

The boxes were full of pajamas. People across the country had read the article and sent her pajamas. *Thousands* of pajamas. "Every day for about a month these boxes just kept filling up the lobby," she says. "My husband and I brought each one of them up to our little one-bedroom apartment. We didn't have room for anything else."

What had happened? Why had a short article in a magazine triggered such an incredible response? "These people just felt that this little gesture—giving a child pajamas—was *so* important," Genevieve says. "One old lady sent me the money she usually used to buy bread, so I could buy more pajamas for the kids."

After that, things snowballed. Genevieve's program was granted not-for-profit status, which helped it really take off. Then she picked up the phone one day and heard two sentences she will never forget: "Hi, I'm a producer with *Oprah*. Do you have a minute to talk?"

❧

Oprah invited Genevieve to tell her story on the show in 2010. The theme of the episode was the question, "What is your calling?"

"This is what I know for sure," Oprah said at the beginning of the episode. "Everybody comes to our beautiful planet Earth to do something great, something unique, something that only you were born to do."

Genevieve sat next to Oprah onstage and told the story of the Pajama Program—the moment on the subway, the little girl, the 85,000 pairs of pajamas she'd managed to give children in the five years since she started the program.

Then Oprah knocked her socks off.

"We challenged this studio audience to pay it forward and bring as many new pajamas as they could," Oprah told a very surprised Genevieve. But there was a catch—each of the two hundred or so audience members could buy only one pair of pajamas themselves. They also had to persuade as many other people as they could to buy and donate pajamas. Oprah herself had no idea how many pajamas had been brought in, until a producer came onstage and handed her an envelope. Oprah opened it and held it up so everyone could see the number of donated pajamas.

A few hundred? A thousand? Five thousand?

No.

In all, there were *32,046 pajamas.*

Staffers wheeled out giant bins overflowing with new pajamas. Genevieve was shocked and couldn't stop crying.

"People really want to help and often just don't know what

to do," Oprah told Genevieve and the studio audience. "You all showed them what to do."

※

The Pajama Program has been in operation for fifteen years now, and so far they have given children *more than four million pairs of pajamas.*

The program has sixty-four chapters and helps children in all fifty states. It has opened three reading centers and plans to open more. And there is a small but growing army of volunteers nationwide that helps implement the plan that, like a raindrop, dropped into Genevieve's brain on a subway.

There are also the children—the many tens of thousands of children who received new pajamas from Genevieve and her army.

"There is one girl named Teresa who came to us when she was two years old," Genevieve says. "Her mother was caught up in drugs and they couldn't be reunited, so she wound up in foster care. She is fifteen now, and she is doing really well in school, and she has a scholarship fund for college. And she came to one of our events recently and talked about how she remembered being in her new pajamas when she was little, and how much she loved to read and have us read to her. It was incredibly touching."

As Genevieve points out, there is research showing that the comfort of bedtime, and the experience of one-on-one reading, is hugely important for children.

"A pajama is so much more than just a piece of cloth," she says. "It means comfort; it means compassion. It means security. Nighttime is scary for children; there are monsters and school bullies and all these frightening things for them to worry about. And so a pajama is a kind of hug. It all comes down to love."

For Genevieve, the path to discovering her true purpose wasn't easy. There was never enough money to keep things running, and there were lots of sleepless nights spent wondering how she'd make it.

But Genevieve didn't allow those fears and doubts to stop her from taking action.

"A lot of people scare themselves out of making a change," she says. "They have kids in school and other obligations, and all these things stop them. But you will never be truly at peace if you are not following your purpose. So think about it. Believe that you are here for something bigger than just a job. Keep asking every day to be pointed in the right direction. Because if you feel there is something missing, then there is."

A moment of introspection, followed by more introspection, followed by people calling her crazy, followed by Oprah and four million pajamas.

And now an invisible thread connects Genevieve to *all* the children who have worn her pajamas, and felt her love, and given *her* something she needed, too. A path. A calling. A purpose.

A way to be an angel on earth.

LOOK FOR THE ANGEL

I used to think the biggest leap of faith on the day I met Maurice was my decision to take him to lunch.

The last five years have taught me I was wrong.

The biggest leap of faith that day was something Maurice did.

You see, I could have just given him money; after all, that's what he'd asked me for. But instead I said, "Maurice, is it okay if I go to lunch with you?"

Maurice was only eleven, but he was incredibly street-smart. He'd lived in more than twenty different shelters and welfare hotels before I met him. He knew he had to be suspicious of everyone. If he wasn't, he might not survive. Drug dealers, social workers, police—everyone wanted something. Everyone had an angle. In his world, no one was kind just to be kind. So he never let anyone in.

And yet—

Maurice allowed me to join him for lunch.

Today, Maurice will tell you it was his growling stomach—he hadn't had anything to eat for two days when we met—that caused him to lower his defenses and accept my invitation to lunch.

But the truth is, he didn't have to let me join him. He could have just asked for the money or for the food. Instead, he invited me into his life, even if just for an hour or so. And that's what allowed an invisible thread to take hold.

Despite everything he'd been taught, Maurice saw the angel in me.

On a basic level, seeing the angel in one another means paying more attention to our similarities than to our differences.

For instance, if someone cuts in front of you at the supermarket checkout line, don't just get mad and curse them under your breath.

Instead, try imagining why they did it. Imagine why you would do it.

It could be because they're a jerk. But it could be something else.

Maybe they're in a hurry to be with their kids, whom they haven't seen all day. Maybe they're not feeling well. Maybe they're worried about a million problems and weren't paying attention.

The point is, try seeing the good in them. Broaden the lens you use to look at the world. Be clearer in how you observe people.

Because if you do, you just might find an angel instead of a jerk.

THE GARDEN

Monique Cano's goal was to be the cranky old neighborhood lady.

She and her husband were living in a small house they'd recently bought in a suburban subdivision near Chicago. The house was in a cul-de-sac close to a park, and the local kids—some from poorer sections of town—would ride around her property and cut through her lawn on the way to the park. "I just didn't want them bothering me," Monique says. "I didn't want to associate with them. I was worried about vandalism and about my dog chasing after them. So I wound up putting up a big fence."

The problem was, Monique wasn't really cranky. And she wasn't old. She was just thirty-two. She did have a metaphorical wall around her—"Heck, it was like I had alligators and piranhas around me," she says—but that really wasn't her nature, either. It was just how she chose to protect herself in her new neighborhood, around new people.

This is a story about how Monique's wall came crumbling down.

She was working in the garden in her front lawn one afternoon when she heard the local boys on their bikes racing nearby. All of a sudden, one of the boys—tall, skinny, nine years old—fell behind his friends and stopped on his bike just a few feet from where Monique was digging up dirt. For a while the boy just stood there, straddling his bicycle. Monique tried to ignore him. Finally, he spoke.

"Can I help?" the boy asked.

"No," Monique said quickly and curtly.

The boy shrugged and rode off on his bike.

The next afternoon, when Monique was in her garden again, the boy came back.

"Can I help?" he asked once more.

"Uh, no," Monique said, more firmly than the last time.

The same thing happened the next day, and the day after that. Still, the boy kept coming back.

Then, one afternoon, he pulled up on his bicycle and asked Monique if he could help yet again. This time, Monique stopped digging and looked up at the boy.

"If you want," she said. "I'm really not doing anything fun, but if you want to help, then okay."

The boy got off his bicycle and stepped into the garden.

$$\approx\!\approx$$

What changed?

"It was his shoes," Monique recalls. "I'd seen the boy before, and he always had on the same pair of black and orange Nike sneakers. And when he came up to me, I could see his big toes poking out of the sneakers. I could see the soles were worn through. He was even walking funny. It made me think, 'This boy could use a friend.'"

Monique wasn't doing much actual gardening. Instead, she was clearing away dirt that had been dumped over her grass when she'd had her fence put up. She gave the boy a little shovel, and he got down and started clearing the dirt with her.

"What's your name?" she asked.

"James," he said.

"Hi, James. I'm Monique."

After that, Monique's wall came down very quickly.

"I asked him about school and his family and his friends," she says. "We spent about an hour in the garden just talking and moving dirt around. It wasn't exciting, but he was so happy to do it. I got the feeling he was glad to be away from the other kids for a while."

Monique would later learn that James, who was tall for his age but also scrawny, was routinely beat up and mocked because of his old shoes and dirty clothes.

The next day, James was back in front of her garden, asking if he could help. He became her regular helper, and her friend. One day, instead of gardening, Monique took him to the local Target and had him pick out a new pair of shoes. "His old ones were size two," she says. "When we fitted him for new ones, they were size five."

Bit by bit, Monique learned about James's family. His mother had four children with three different fathers, none of whom were around. She was also caring for her older sister who was blind and mute. James no longer lived with her, and instead he was staying with his grandmother and two sisters in a house on the street behind where Monique lived. "His mother really had her hands full," Monique says. "She seemed like a good mom, but she just didn't have time for James."

But Monique did. Together they landscaped her front lawn, and one day James even showed up with a bunch of seeds in his palm. "I had no idea where he got them from, but he knew I loved my garden, so he brought them for me," she says. "They turned out to be for a really unique, exotic plant. We planted the seeds, and when they came up, he tended to the little plants when he was around."

Monique helped James with his homework. She taught him how to cook. He showed up with a kite one afternoon, and—despite whipping winds—Monique agreed to try to fly it with him. "He got it from a teacher and he was so excited about it," she says. "But it was this cheap kite and it fell apart right away."

One afternoon, James was waiting for her when she pulled into her driveway. He seemed unusually quiet. Monique told him she needed to make a phone call and asked him to come back in twenty minutes. But just twenty seconds later, he knocked on her door. She opened it and saw him crying.

"My bike got stolen," he said.

Monique is only five feet tall, but she's a lot tougher than she looks. She rides a motorcycle, and she earned a reputation in her community as the woman who could fix things—the mayor of the subdivision. When she heard James's bike had been stolen, she walked outside with him and said, "Let's go."

A couple of blocks over, she saw two of the boys James usually rode with.

"You have five minutes to return his bike," she told them.

"I don't know what you're talking about," one of them said.

"I have a security camera," she said—when, in fact, she didn't. "I know you know where the bike is. You have five minutes, starting now."

Two minutes later, James's bicycle was back in her driveway.

※

On another afternoon, one of Monique's neighbors came over and said, "You'd better go check on James."

Monique found him in another part of the subdivision. Two policemen were there, and so was his mother. James was bleeding and subdued.

"He had been beaten up pretty badly by two older girls," Monique says. "He didn't fight back because they were girls. I asked the police officers to drive over to where the girls were and just let me see them."

"Who are you?" one of the officers asked dismissively.

Before she could answer, Monique heard a voice.

"She's his godmother, that's who she is."

It was James's mother.

Monique was shocked. She had never even spoken to James's mother before. From the look on his face, James was shocked, too. The police officer nodded and drove off in the direction of the girls.

An hour later, Monique and James were sitting on her side deck, talking.

"What's a godmother?" James asked.

"Well, a godmother is someone who looks after you and takes care of you when you need it," she said.

James thought about that for a moment.

"Kind of like you?" he finally said.

"Yeah," Monique said, fighting back tears, "kind of like me."

After that, James never called her anything except god-momma.

They spent two years together, gardening, talking, being friends. But then Monique's marriage fell apart, and she got a divorce. She also decided to move a short drive away. "James was very upset about the divorce, and he asked me if I was okay," she says. "He was worried about my feelings. But he was also upset that I was moving. We'd still be able to see each other, but it wouldn't be the same."

The two friends did continue to hang out together, just less so. Eventually, Monique remarried and had a child of her own. Still, she stayed in touch with James and invited him to her son's birthday parties. She also made sure to bring him a gift when it was his birthday. One year, she gave him a present that was big but unusually light. James ripped off the wrapping paper and finally figured out what it was.

It was a kite.

A good, sturdy kite, fashioned like a hawk, with sleek lines and bright colors.

James stared at it for a while and then looked up at Monique.

"You remembered," is all he said.

"He was more excited that I'd remembered than he was about the kite," Monique says. "Remembering meant someone cared about him. We took the kite out to the field, and this time it flew really high in the sky. He was so, so happy."

James is fourteen now, and Monique and her husband, Michael, still see him when they can. They bring him along on family picnics, have him over to swim in the pool and bounce on the trampoline, and recently let him tag along to a big motorcycle gathering. James is smart and determined, and he wants to join the Army one day and become an Army Ranger. "I always told him he could do whatever he wanted in life, but that he had to have a goal," Monique says. "I still tell him every time I see him that he can be whoever he wants, and I believe that. I want him to succeed. I want him to excel. I want to make sure he has a really good life."

Theirs is an unlikely friendship, between a woman who wanted to be the nasty neighborhood lady and a wild street kid who really wasn't. It began in a tiny little garden, and it grew from there into something beautiful. And it grew because James saw the angel in Monique before she saw it in herself.

"I mean, I told him no *so* many times," Monique says. "I was trying to keep him away. I was trying to be that cranky old lady. I *wanted* to be that lady! But James saw through it. He saw that wasn't who I was. Instead, when he looked at me, he saw a friend. Somehow, he knew that before I did."

And once Monique's wall came crumbling down, it never went back up.

THROW OUT THE RULE BOOK

Here is an angel on earth story I love.

I read about it in USA Today, and it involves a North Carolina high school football coach named Wayne Inman and an often-suspended, headed-for-trouble freshman named Dwayne Allen. One day, the coach ran into the freshman in a hallway and asked him if he'd ever played football. Dwayne said he hadn't. Then Wayne handed him a ten-dollar bill.

"Buy yourself a bag of dope," the coach told the freshman, "or spend it on a physical and come on out for football."

Dwayne used the ten dollars on a physical. He tried out for the football team and made it.

A few years later, he was playing in the National Football League.

A tiny moment became a turning point.

What's great about this story for me is the unconventional method Coach Inman used to make a connection. He didn't just offer ten dollars—he offered a challenge. And that challenge, Dwayne would later say, "changed my life."

Sometimes, to be an angel on earth, we have to take chances. Go against convention. Throw out the rule book. Disregard warnings.

Because kindness doesn't come with an instruction manual.

26

THE WARNING

"That family is nothing but trouble."

Those were the first words Mary Warwick heard about a boy in her kindergarten class named Terrance. "He had a lot of brothers and sisters come through here, and they were all trouble," the vice principal told her. "Watch out for him."

Mary had just recently earned her teaching certificate, and this was her first class. She grew up an Air Force brat and lived all over—Florida, Okinawa, Colorado, Mississippi. Her first love was animals, so she trained to be a veterinary technician and worked at the Houston Zoo. But something also drew her toward teaching. "I decided I wanted to influence children," Mary says. "So I earned my bachelor's in education and received my certificate, and I found a job at an elementary school outside Houston."

There were twenty-two children in her kindergarten class, including Terrance, who was six. Mary's first impression of him was that he was shy and quiet. But then, on one of the first days of class, while the children were split up into separate activity groups, Mary heard a commotion. It was Terrance. "Someone took something from him, and Terrance just blew up," she says. "I was shocked. He was cursing and screaming and pushing the boy. I had him sit in time-out for five minutes. Then I spoke with him about how he could have handled the situation differently."

After five minutes, Terrance rejoined the group, and the rest of the day went fine. But the next day, he blew up again. During her first week, Terrance lost his temper several times. "He just had these terrible outbursts," Mary says. "He would curse at the children and sometimes punch them and knock them over. It was disruptive, and his behavior was unacceptable. I would sit him down and work out a plan for a better way for him to deal with confrontations. But the outbursts continued."

When the vice principal warned Mary about Terrance, he also told her the protocol for unruly children. If the time-outs didn't work, "I was supposed to send them to the principal's office," says Mary. "I finally did that with Terrance, but even then I thought, 'How is he supposed to learn if he's in the principal's office every day?'"

The trips to see the principal didn't help. Terrance's outbursts only got worse.

One day, Terrance and some other children were in an activity center playing with blocks. One of the other children knocked over Terrance's blocks, and that set him off. "He really flew off the handle this time," says Mary. "He was really angry, and he cursed at a boy and pushed him down. It was his worst blowup."

At the time, Mary was sitting cross-legged on the floor, tending to another group of children. But she was close enough to Terrance to reach out and grab him. In that instant, Mary didn't think about the protocol. She just acted.

"I reached over and I grabbed Terrance and I pulled him in and I gave him a hug," she says. "I pulled him toward me and just hugged him. It was all instinct. I did everything I wasn't supposed to. But when I hugged Terrance he didn't fight me at all. He just fell into the hug."

The hug didn't solve Terrance's problems. "But it did establish something between us," Mary says. "His outbursts continued, but as the year went on he got better. He began to open up to me about his family. He understood that I cared about him and that I was there for him."

When spring rolled around, the students had to sign up for the spring sports they were interested in. Most of the boys said they were signing up to play T-ball, but Terrance didn't say a word. "I could tell he was confused, as if he was thinking, 'Why don't I get to play T-ball?'" Mary says. "After class I asked him if he wanted to play, and he got very excited and said yes." Mary took it upon herself to go to Terrance's home and get his parents to sign the necessary release. "It was a bad neighborhood," she says. "There were all these people in the house, maybe a dozen of them. I later found out his mother was dealing drugs out of the house." Mary couldn't find Terrance's mother that day, but she did find his father and got him to sign the release.

Playing T-ball was a huge success for Terrance. "He loved it so much and he did so well," says Mary. "A couple of times he was awarded the game ball. I could see the joy on his face when I watched him play. What he loved most about it was the *normalcy*. And he never had a single outburst on the field."

For family reasons, Mary left the elementary school after one year. But she stayed in touch with Terrance and became his un-official mentor. She went to the library with him and helped him with math, and she pushed him to do his homework and prepare for tests. "He was basically all on his own," says Mary. "He didn't have a clock or a watch, so he was always late. When he was in kindergarten I got him a clock, but it was stolen." When Terrance was in the third grade, his coaches and teammates' parents began helping get Terrance to his baseball practices and games.

One afternoon after school, Mary went to Terrance's home to take him to the library. When she got there, she ran into Terrance's mother. Mary mentioned something about how much better Terrance was doing.

"If you like him so much I can sell him to you," his mother replied.

Mary was shocked. So, she figured, was Terrance, who was right there when his mother offered to sell him. Later that day, she sat him down and they talked about what had happened. "I told him his mother had a sickness and she didn't know what she was saying. Terrance understood this, but I could tell he was really hurt."

When Terrance was in the fourth grade, Mary drove to his house to pick him up for another outing. She knocked on the front door, but no one answered. The door was open, so she looked inside. No one was there. All the furniture was gone. The house was completely empty.

"I walked through it, looking for some sign of what had happened," she says. "And in the corner, I found one of Terrance's baseball trophies broken on the floor."

Someone had gotten in trouble with the law, and the family had fled town. Terrance was nowhere to be found. In the weeks and months that followed, Mary kept driving by his house, hoping to see him. But she never did. One day, Mary spotted a sign in front of the house that read, CONDEMNED. A few weeks later, when she drove by again, the house was gone altogether.

Mary didn't hear from Terrance for the next five years.

Until, finally, he called.

~~~

"Hi, Mrs. Warwick," Terrance said, because that's what he'd always called her.

"Hi, Terrance," Mary said, trying to hold back her tears.

His family had taken him first to Georgia and then to Louisiana, and his situation hadn't improved. He was older now, and the lure of the streets was stronger. He was in danger of getting sucked into the family business—drugs. But he'd never lost the phone number that Mary had given him, and he started calling her once a month just to talk. In one of their conversations, Terrance mentioned he'd dropped out of school. "When he got to Louisiana he was way behind all the other students, and he just said, 'I can't catch up,'" she says. "That's when I really started to worry. He was a kid on the streets now."

One of Terrance's next calls to Mary was from jail.

"He was arrested for selling drugs. He was embarrassed about it and worried that I would be disappointed. And I was, but I also understood that he got pulled into the lifestyle. I felt so powerless."

Mary paid for an attorney and went to Louisiana for Terrance's trial. She wasn't sure she'd even recognize him in the courtroom, but when she saw him, he smiled at her and she smiled back. "He looked like the same little kid I hugged," she says.

The judge sentenced Terrance to probation, on the condition that he return to Houston with Mary. "I was excited because, if he came with me, I felt I could really help him," she says. It would take some time for Terrance to be released from jail, so they agreed to meet at the courthouse right before he was let go. Mary showed up early and waited for Terrance to come out. A half hour passed, then an hour. Mary waited for three hours, but still no sign of Terrance. "I finally asked about him, and they said he had been released hours ago and slipped out a back door. I went back to Houston alone."

Terrance eventually called to apologize and explained he'd

wanted to stay in Louisiana to take care of his ailing father. Just a few months later, though, Mary got another call from him.

He was in jail again.

"This time there was nothing I could do to help," Mary says. "I called the attorney, but Terrance had violated probation, and they were going to keep him in jail." In fact, he was given a four-year sentence, with no chance of early release. In that time, not a single member of Terrance's family ever went to see him.

The only real contact he had with anyone on the outside were his weekly phone calls with Mary.

"I would send him books and CDs, and I worried about him every night," Mary says. "The funny thing is, Terrance never felt sorry for himself. He was never looking for pity. He accepted what he had done, and he promised me that when he got out, he would never go anywhere near drugs again." One day, Mary opened a letter from Terrance and saw he'd written her a poem. It was titled, simply, "Thank You."

"Just cross your heart and hope that I make it," Terrance wrote. "And know that my love for you will remain untainted."

———※———

In prison, Terrance managed to earn his GED. When he finally got out, the terms of his release prevented him from leaving the state of Louisiana, so he couldn't move near or even visit Mary and her family. So they did what they'd been doing for so many years: they talked over the phone. "He calls all the time to let me know how he's doing, and I can tell he is really, really trying to make something of himself," she says. "He desperately wants to break the cycle of drugs and violence that he's been caught in, but there are just so many forces working against him. It's going to be incredibly hard."

Terrance is twenty-seven now and still trying to break the cycle. His dream is to be a welder, and he's doing what he can to make it come true. Mary helped him finally get his social security card and driver's license, but there are other challenges, other obstacles. In the meantime, he takes whatever jobs he can find. "I still have so much hope for him," says Mary. "I hope that something will change, something will turn around for him. But Terrance is an adult, and he understands it is up to him now. All I can do is let him know I am here for him."

It's been more than twenty years since Mary ignored the protocol and gave Terrance a hug. Since then, his journey has been difficult and painful. As for his future, no one can possibly know.

But one thing is certain—and unchanging.

Mary will always be connected to Terrance.

"At the end of every call he always says, 'I love you, Mrs. Warwick,' and I always say, 'I love you, too, Terrance,' and that's how it will always be," Mary says. "No matter what, Terrance knows that someone loves him, someone cares about him, someone will always pick up the phone when he calls. It's something I tell him every time we talk: 'Terrance, you and I are in this life together.'"

A GOD CONNECTION

I have a special connection to my friend Mary Phillips.

Long ago, Mary's older sister Kathy worked with my older sister Annette. It so happened that Mary and I were both moving to New York City at around the same time, and our sisters thought we should meet. When I finally called Mary, I asked her where she worked.

"On Fifty-first Street and Fifth Avenue," she said.

"Fifty-first and Fifth? That's where I work, too!"

Turns out Mary was on the east side of the street, and I was on the west side. Then we continued to chat and I asked her where she lived.

"I'm on Eighty-third Street between First and Second avenues," Mary said.

"Wait a minute. I'm on Eighty-third between First and Second, too!"

Turns out we were just two buildings apart.

Instantly, we knew we would be friends.

As our friendship grew, there were other parallels. We both had two sisters and two brothers. Neither of us ended up having children of our own. And we both loved little dogs.

My first lovely little canine angel was a red French poodle named Lucy, and then two more poodles named Coco and Emma. Meanwhile, Mary spent nearly all her adult life without any pets. Still, she always knew that if she ever did get a dog, she wanted it to be a little white dog—a bichon or maybe a poodle.

Which brings me to the point of this story.

Mary's busy life—she worked in Manhattan, got married, moved to Connecticut, got divorced, worked as a Realtor—eventually led her to

Florida, where her good friend Darlene had a big chocolate Lab named Lady. Now, Lady loved Mary. "She was blind, and she'd hear my voice and start walking toward me and bump into everything because she couldn't see, until she finally reached me and sort of banged into me, the poor thing," says Mary. "It was Lady who started me thinking about finally getting a dog of my own."

Then a couple of strange things happened. Mary was headed to church on Sunday when Darlene called her. "We didn't usually go to church together, but that Sunday she just happened to want to come with me," says Mary.

Then the minister gave a sermon that included a story about dogs.

"He was a big dog lover, and he gave this beautiful talk about the love and the joy that dogs bring and the responsibility of caring for them," says Mary. "It was a really moving message about love."

After the service, outside the church, Mary turned to Darlene and said, "I think I'm ready to start looking for a dog."

"Great!" Darlene said. "Let's start going to the animal shelters."

But they never made it to a single shelter.

That very night, Darlene and her Lab, Lady, went for a walk on Jupiter Beach. As they were strolling, Darlene saw a woman approaching with a little dog in her arms. The dog was scruffy and scraggly, with dirty, matted hair. The two women stopped to talk, and Darlene asked about the dog.

"She's not mine," the woman said. "She's my neighbor's dog. They don't want her and I volunteered to find her a good home."

Darlene couldn't believe what she was hearing. Though the dog's hair was filthy and she'd clearly been neglected, Darlene could tell one thing about her. She was a bichon.

"Don't do anything," Darlene told the woman. "Let me call my friend."

Later that evening, Darlene and Mary drove to the neighbor's house to see the bichon. When Mary sat down and held the dog, her life changed. "She made this incredible eye contact with me," Mary says. "After that, it was over. I was in love."

The little white dog—her name was Annabella—did indeed become Mary's dog. But not just a dog. "We did everything together," she says. "She was a great traveler and we would take long drives to see my mother and stepdad, and Bella would sit in the passenger seat and we'd share little snacks. She slept with me in my bed, and when I watched TV at night she sat in the ottoman right next to me. We learned how to communicate—she'd stare at me and lick her lips once and I knew that meant she was hungry. It was like we'd been together forever."

Finding Bella the way she did, Mary believes, was no accident. "To me, Bella was a gift from God," she says. "Going to church with Darlene, and then the sermon about dogs, and then Darlene running into Bella on the beach—that is a God connection. I'm not saying it's a miracle. But it's definitely not an accident, either."

When I wrote An Invisible Thread, I believed these special connections happened only between two people. But the last five years have taught me how wrong I was. After Mary shared her story with me, and after so many others wrote to describe their invisible thread connections with animals they love, I came to understand that, just as people are put in one another's paths precisely when they need each other, so, too, can animals appear in our lives at just the right moment.

27

THE RABBIT

Lucy Galasso has loved animals for as long as she can remember. Her father was a superintendent on a large estate in Connecticut, and growing up she was surrounded by ducks, pigeons, chickens, and dogs. "I carried that love with me forever," she says, "but when my daughter was born, I sort of put it on the back burner."

That is, until her daughter turned eight, and Lucy bought a horse for her to ride. "He was this lovely, pure white Welsh cross named Pony Express," she says. "We called him Poe. My daughter loved riding him and took him with her to college, and together they won awards in competitions."

After that, the animals just kept coming. Currently, Lucy, who lives with her husband, Alan, on a beautiful five acres named Sunny Meadows in the town of Bedford, New York, has some thirty animals. "Let's see, I have two horses, a miniature cow, six sheep, two goats, ten chickens, four ducks, a turkey, two cats, and a little terrier mix," she says. "It's not a working farm or anything like that. They're just all my pets."

From time to time, Lucy would travel to see an animal breeder in Carmel, New York, to add a few new members to her menagerie. "I drove up there one day to buy some chickens," she says. "I picked some out and I was leaving the property and getting into my car when the breeder suddenly said, 'Hold on.'"

Just outside the main house, there was a little cage sitting on the ground. The breeder looked at Lucy and pointed at the cage.

"By the way," she said, "I have this bunny for free, if you want him."

"Why for free?" Lucy asked.

"'Cause no one wants him."

Lucy went over to the cage and looked in. She saw a small Dutch rabbit, black with a white collar, white paws, and a white nose. The breeder took the rabbit out of the cage and handed him to Lucy.

"He fit perfectly in my arms," she says. "I fell in love with him right away."

Then Lucy drove home with her new chickens and her free bunny rabbit.

His name was Jack, and he was very smart. Lucy set him up in a hutch on her property, and he fit right in with the rest of the gang. One day a neighbor called to say she'd just seen three of Lucy's animals march by her window in single file: her bulldog, Tara, followed by her potbellied pig, Mimi, followed by Jack the Rabbit. "She thought it was adorable," Lucy says of her neighbor. "But that was Jack. He was a character."

At the time, Lucy was working as a social studies teacher at an alternative high school. "It was for bright kids who for different reasons were having trouble learning," she says. "Square pegs in round holes." It wasn't easy for Lucy to get through to her students; they could be closed off, angry, belligerent. "I was always asking myself, 'How do you teach kids like this? How do you make it more creative for them?'"

Then she was asked to teach a class in psychology. One assignment had to do with positive and negative reinforcement. It was then that Lucy had a lightbulb moment. "The lesson was all about training behavior," she says. "And I just thought, 'I know! I'll bring in my bunnies!'"

Lucy had noticed that one of the few things that truly captured her students' attention was a discussion about animals. Many of them had pets, and when she talked to them about their pets, she could see their guards coming down. "One of my most difficult kids was this young girl who had a bad attitude and a problem with drugs," Lucy says. "She had to figure me out before she could trust me and accept me. I heard that she had a ferret, so I sat down with her one day to talk to her about it. It was clear she really adored that ferret, and we wound up having lots of long discussions. That's how I won her over."

The logical next step? Bring in the bunnies!

"I didn't have to run it past any administrators," Lucy says. "They just sort of let me do my own thing, which was lucky, I guess."

Lucy had four rabbits: Jack plus three friendly lop-eared rabbits. She brought them to school in cages and divided her students into four groups. "The assignment was to train your rabbit to do a trick," Lucy says. "It could be walking from here to there. Or jumping through a hoop. The idea was to figure out how to get the rabbit to do something."

Lucy's students lit up. She thought they might enjoy the rabbits, but they responded to them in a way she'd never expected. "They were so animated," she says. "I saw a spark in them I'd never seen before."

Finally, it was time for each group to demonstrate what they'd taught their rabbit. One group used bits of alfalfa to lure a rabbit down a little walkway. Another group got their rabbit to jump through a hoop. Then Lucy got to the group that was training Jack. She watched as Jack hopped down a little walkway. Next, he jumped through the hoop, too.

But Jack wasn't done then, either.

"Somehow, these kids had taught Jack to get up on his hind legs and *give them a high five!*" she says. "A high five with his little paw! I couldn't believe my eyes!"

It was, Lucy says now, her finest and most memorable moment as a teacher. "Jack really wowed those kids," she says. "He got me through a very difficult time with my students. They loved him, and they loved coming to class to see him. I even let them take Jack home on weekends."

Jack changed the way Lucy approached teaching. She began to encourage her students to bring their own pets to school on certain days, and she saw the profound effect animals could have on troubled youngsters. "I had one really pugnacious student who always seemed to be angry," Lucy says. "One day a dog was visiting with his owner, and I asked the student to walk the dog around the school building. I looked out the window and watched them together, and it was amazing. They were running and playing fetch and having a great time. The dog really got through to him, and his anger dissipated. The animals were worth their weight in gold."

That was the only semester Lucy taught a psychology class, and she never brought Jack in for any other lesson. "They heard about him on the main campus, though, and they asked me to bring him in for a class on animal behavior," she says. "He became known as the rabbit who gave his students high fives."

Lucy did bring other animals into class—a sweet little duck

named Alex, a funny rooster named Walter—and the result was always the same: happy, engaged students. Jack, meanwhile, enjoyed his retirement from the rigors of academia by hopping around the house and sitting in Lucy's lap while she graded homework.

One morning, Lucy went to Jack's hutch to feed him his usual pellets and cracked corn. She found him lying peacefully on the ground.

"He had passed," Lucy says. "He was seven. That's the average life span for Dutch rabbits. He never slowed down; that's not how it happens. I just went out there and found him."

Near the front of her property, there are several trees that give shade to a little stretch of grass and dirt. Over the years, this little stretch became the resting place for Lucy's babies. She found a small metallic angel with wings at a tag sale, and she bought it and laid it on top of Jack's spot, not far from a tree, in the peaceful shade.

"It felt right," Lucy says. "Jack the Rabbit was my angel. And he was an angel to all those kids who needed him."

SEE INTO THE FUTURE

A few months after my first lunch with Maurice, I invited him to come with me to my sister Annette's house on Long Island.

My sister Annette, her husband, Bruce, and their three children, Colette, Derek, and Brooke had all heard about Maurice, and they were excited to meet him. When we arrived, Maurice ran off to play on the swings with the children and ride bikes with Derek. Then it was time for dinner, and we all sat around the big dining room table. Everyone was laughing and talking and passing food back and forth.

Driving back to New York City, I asked a sleepy Maurice, "What was your favorite part of the day?" I expected him to say the swings or the bike ride or some other fun activity. But Maurice's answer surprised me.

"I loved the room with the big table," he said.

The dining room? His favorite thing? When I thought about it, I understood. Maurice wasn't used to sitting at a table to eat. In his world, everyone ate wherever and whenever they had food—if they had food. He wasn't used to a family talking and laughing and sharing love across a big table.

"Miss Laura," Maurice said that night, "when I get older, I'm gonna have a room and a big table just like that, where me and my family can eat."

That was another first for Maurice and me.

It was the first time I'd ever heard Maurice talk about his future—his first dream about a life beyond the one he had.

Living your life with clearness means seeing into the future. To be an angel on earth, you have to see what isn't there—the potential, the possibilities, the beauty of what can be.

Again, it's about perception: Is reality what exists right now, or what can exist if we step in and change it?

Oh, and today, Maurice does have a big dining room table in his apartment—where his lovely wife, Michelle, and their seven amazing children like to hang out and talk and laugh and share lots of love.

————————————————————

28

THE SUNBURN

Angel Pérez was born in Puerto Rico and raised in the South
Bronx. When he got there at the age of three—"my parents
were looking for economic opportunities and a better life," he
says—the South Bronx wasn't just a dangerous place to live. It
was seen as *the* most dangerous place to live.

The South Bronx was the national symbol of urban decay, with
blocks and blocks of burned-out buildings, rampant drugs and violence, and crushing poverty. Street gangs, squatters, drug addicts,
thieves—the area was essentially a failed, forgotten neighborhood. "One of my first memories is living in low-income housing
and waking up with rats around me," Angel recalls. "When my
brother was born he got the crib, to protect him from the rats, and
I had to sleep in the hallway."

When Angel was in middle school, he was held up at knifepoint
just a couple of blocks from school. At thirteen he was mugged for
his winter jacket by eight teenagers and sent to the hospital with
a broken arm, cuts and bruises, and a bloodshot eye. One day, he
was walking in his building's courtyard when he heard a gunshot.

"I ran and scrambled and I looked up and someone was lying
on the ground, dead," Angel says. "That stayed with me for a long
time. I was afraid to play outside. I was always on edge, thinking it
could happen to me. I didn't get the chance to be a kid."

It seemed inevitable that he would attend South Bronx High School near where he lived. But he entered a lottery for a spot in Martin Luther King, Jr. High School in Manhattan, near Lincoln Center. In the 1970s, that area was also beset by drugs and gangs and violence, but at least it was better than the Bronx. To his great relief, Angel was accepted into the school. "I knew I didn't want to spend the rest of my life in the South Bronx," he says. "So getting into MLK was step one."

Angel took two trains and a bus every morning to get to school. The threat of being mugged or attacked was still there, so Angel joined as many after-school programs as he could to avoid leaving at 3:00 p.m., when all the schools in the area let out. "I didn't do all those extra activities to build a portfolio for college," he says with a laugh. "I did them so I wouldn't get beat up."

One of his activities was the student mediator program, which enlisted certain students to mediate disputes and deliver a resolution to the guidance counselors. Angel prepared one such resolution and ran over to the offices of the guidance counselors to present it. When he got there, the scene was pure chaos. "This was a school of four thousand kids, and there weren't that many counselors," he says. "There were a ton of kids there, and it was just crazy. I had to wait patiently until one of the counselors was free."

Angel finally went in to see a counselor in her thirties named Irma.

He hadn't met Irma yet, but he knew her by sight. "She was of German descent, with very blonde hair," he says. "She used to be a gymnast, so the way she carried herself was striking. She didn't really look like anyone else at the school. You looked at her and you had to wonder, 'What is this woman doing here?'"

Irma motioned for Angel to come in. He gave her the resolution and waited while she read it over. Then she looked up and smiled.

"This is fantastic," she said. "What's your name?"

"Angel Pérez, ma'am."

"Angel, you need to come back and see me," Irma said. "We need to talk about your future."

~~~≪≫~~~

Something about Angel had impressed her. Maybe it was that he was polite and respectful. Or that he was so well spoken. Whatever the reason, Irma took a special interest in him. "The thing is, she wasn't even my guidance counselor," Angel says. "I had a different counselor, and Irma already had five hundred other kids she was in charge of. But she took an interest in me anyway."

Still, Angel had a choice: he could either go back to see Irma, or he could decide not to. He decided to go back. "In a building where you have thousands of kids, you don't get much personal attention," he says, recalling his decision. "And we all need that. We all need someone to pay attention to us. The fact that Irma didn't know me and was still nice to me drew me in. It was a simple expression of kindness, but it had a big impact on me."

Angel began stopping by to visit Irma whenever he could. They would talk about his schoolwork, his future, and his life. "If you looked at us, we were probably the two least likely people to have anything in common," he says, "and yet we talked about everything. She asked me a lot of questions about my life and my story."

One spring Sunday, Angel and his friends played outside for hours. He came back home with a serious sunburn. "I showed up to school on Monday as red as a cherry tomato," he says. A little later that day, Irma found him in the hallway and handed him a small bottle.

It was aloe vera lotion for his sunburn.

"At first, I was confused," says Angel. "I wondered, 'Why did she do that?' Here is this woman, she's not my counselor, she has no obligation to help me in any way, and certainly not to spend money on me, and yet she did it anyway."

The lotion probably cost five dollars. But when Irma gave it to Angel, he was overwhelmed. "Looking back on it now, that moment allowed me to make a really joyful connection with the world. It gave me hope. Where I came from, no one was nice to each other. Everyone was working a hustle. But Irma was just being kind. It was a small but incredibly powerful gesture."

Only much later did Angel learn that Irma had not been randomly assigned to Martin Luther King, Jr. High School. "Her first teaching job had been on Long Island in a school in a wealthy area, and she'd been miserable," Angel says. "The privilege, the sense of entitlement—she said, 'There's no way I can do this.' So she asked to be transferred to an inner-city school. She said, 'I want to be in a place where I can make a difference.'"

For four years, Angel and Irma continued to meet regularly. She'd help him with his academic schedule. She'd ask, "Why are you taking this math class?" She'd make sure he didn't skip the classes he disliked, and she enrolled him in an after-school tutoring program she'd created. In his senior year, Irma tried to steer Angel toward certain colleges. "She'd say, 'The reps from Skidmore are here—you have to go see them.' She just kept pushing and pushing."

Eventually, Angel applied to a college in New York City, because he wanted to stay near his family. "I had a part-time job that paid seven dollars an hour, and I was going to keep it and go to a college nearby," he says. "I felt guilty about leaving my parents."

But when he told Irma about his plan, "she was beside herself," he says. "She said, 'Oh, no, you are not staying here. You need to apply to bigger and better colleges. You need to get away from home and have a different life.'"

To appease her, Angel applied to schools that were far away, such as Skidmore College in Saratoga Springs, New York. But when he was accepted into Hunter College in New York City, he told Irma he was going there.

"Over my dead body," Irma said. "You are going to Skidmore, even if I have to put your butt on the bus myself."

"But I don't have money for the bus ticket!" Angel protested.

"I will pay for it."

"But I can't leave my family."

"Yes, you can."

Angel was accepted into Skidmore College. He got on the bus to upstate New York. Four years later, he graduated. He was no longer a fearful boy from the Bronx. He was a man ready for life's challenges.

"Those four years," he says, "changed my life."

His parents didn't make it to Angel's college graduation. "I was having a lot of struggles with my father, and he didn't want to go, and my mother didn't want to go without him," Angel says. "But Irma was there."

When he graduated, Angel wasn't sure what kind of job he'd end up with. But he knew one thing: he wanted to work in education, and specifically in the area of helping students map out their futures. "Someone really encouraged me to go to college, and it was a transformative experience," he explains. "I wanted to do that for other young people. I wanted to pay it forward."

Today, Angel is vice president of enrollment and student success at the prestigious Trinity College in Connecticut. He oversees admissions, financial aid, institutional research, career development, and retention. He also teaches courses in the Educational Studies department. In his career, Angel has earned a PhD, been awarded a Fulbright Fellowship, and was named a Master Teacher. He has received many awards, including several for his leadership on behalf of low-income students. "I could never have dreamed of this life for myself," Angel wrote in his email to me, "but one woman who took an interest in me made me believe it was possible."

Irma is retired now and living on Long Island. Angel is still in contact with her, but in a way she is with him every day, as if she were right there beside him. "I had a student at Trinity who was hesitant about studying abroad, and I told her, 'When you get on a plane and go abroad, the world gets smaller,'" Angel says. "And as soon as I said it, I realized those were the *exact words* Irma once told me. I find myself always using the same phrasing with my students today that Irma used with me. She would say, 'You have to take that risk. You have to get on the plane. You have to see the world. You have to *dream bigger.*'"

Angels on earth don't have to move mountains or part the seas. Sometimes, all they have to do is give a little push.

One woman's small gesture of kindness—handing Angel some aloe vera, and in the process showing him a world he didn't know existed—has rippled outward through the years, increasing in strength and power along the way. That legacy of kindness now encompasses the hundreds of students who pass through Angel's office to listen to his words—and the words of a former guidance counselor.

"What I learned from Irma, and what I have learned from working with all those students, is the importance of personal touch, of making that personal connection," Angel says. "All of us feel the need to be validated. Everyone is looking for that, regardless of his or her story. And that validation can be anything. It can be a conversation. It can be an acknowledgment. It can be someone telling you, 'You have something special. You should keep going.'"

Angel says, "It might not seem like much at the time, but it can go a really long way."

PART SEVEN
CONNECTEDNESS

Everyone has invisible thread connections in their lives. We honor and activate those connections through kindness. Honoring our invisible thread connections makes us angels on earth. This is what I've learned from all the stories you've just read. But these final two stories are about the most joyful thing I've learned: That our invisible threads endure beyond this life. That the connectedness that defines us is endless. That angels on earth and angels in heaven aren't really different at all.

29

THE CHILD

His name is Sebastian.

He was born in 2004, two weeks early, almost as if he couldn't wait to get here. His father, Horst Ferrero, a Venezuelan, and his mother, Luisa Cannella Ferrero, whose family is from Italy, picked the name Sebastian because "it is easy to pronounce in English, Spanish, and Italian," Luisa explains. When Sebastian was young and eating in a restaurant, "he would talk to me in Spanish, to Luisa in Italian, and to the waiter in English," says Horst. "He was so confident, so outgoing. He was so full of life."

The bond between the Ferreros and their first child was magical, vibrant. But Sebastian was also becoming a child of the world, open to everyone, connected to all. He had been to three continents and cruised many seas, his life a series of wonderful adventures. "We traveled with him everywhere," says Luisa. "Our goal was to make him feel happy all the time. Not just happy, but *special*."

This was the dream they had for their son—that he grow up to be someone whose love and spirit and energy might one day change the world.

It was a beautiful dream.

Horst and Luisa met on a blind date of sorts. They had common friends who arranged for them to be at the same birthday party. "That night, I told Luisa I loved her smile," remembers Horst, a prominent international lawyer. "I gave her a business card and told her about a seminar I was going to the next day. She said, 'That sounds interesting, I'll look into it.'"

The seminar wound up being booked, but Horst and Luisa met for lunch anyway. Five years later, they were married in a hotel in Venezuela. "It was like an Italian wedding, with lots of family and friends and children," says Luisa, an only child who speaks four languages fluently. In 2003 the Ferreros moved to Gainesville, Florida, and a year later, Sebastian was born. "When they handed him to me for the first time, it was like a miracle," Horst says. "He was our baby, our child."

In the fall of 2007, when Sebastian was three, his pediatrician recommended a procedure called a growth hormone stimulation test because his growth rate was below average for his age. "It was not a treatment or a surgery," says Horst. "It was just a routine test to determine whether he had growth hormone deficiency."

But something went terribly wrong. Sebastian was accidentally overdosed with the natural amino acid used for the test. "It was all very surreal," says Horst, fighting back tears. "Within forty-eight hours, we lost him. Sebastian passed away."

The overdose was caused by a series of preventable errors. "We went through these terrible emotions trying to figure out what had happened," says Luisa, her voice barely a whisper. "It just didn't seem possible." Horst says, "When you lose a child, there is nothing that can bring him back, nothing that can make you feel better. Nothing helps."

The Ferreros felt shock, anguish, sorrow, and confusion. Their loss was unimaginable. In their grief, they could have withdrawn from the world. They could have descended into a well of hopeless bitterness. No one would have blamed them if they had.

But they didn't. They didn't allow themselves to. In the days after the tragedy, "We both realized we couldn't solve anything with frustration and anger," Horst says. "We needed to find a way to help people remember Sebastian. We needed to go forward. We needed a movement, so that Sebastian did not die in vain."

It is one thing to say you want to create a movement. It is easy to dream. But to put the pieces together, to make something actually happen—especially something big and important and unique—isn't easy. It is hugely difficult. It can even seem impossible. For most people, it can be so daunting that they never even take the first step.

Horst and Luisa took the first step.

Their goal was simple: they didn't want any other parents to have to go through what they had gone through. Specifically, they wanted to create a nationally recognized patient safety program that could prevent the kind of errors that had happened in Sebastian's case—and in doing so keep Sebastian's beautiful spirit alive.

Beyond that, they dreamed of creating a state-of-the-art, full-service children's hospital in Gainesville. "With Sebastian, all the hospital services were sprawled out," Luisa says. "The emergency room was mixed with adults and children in one place, and the main hospital and other specialized services were spread around more than a mile away. Those forty-eight hours were an ordeal." Their bold idea was "a hospital for children with everything in one place, under one roof," says Horst. A hospital where children would be safe and protected and given the world's best care.

To make it happen, the Ferreros decided to partner with the very hospital where Sebastian had been accidentally overdosed—the UF Health Shands Hospital.

"We decided we were not going to fight them," Horst says. "They came to us and they were very apologetic. They recognized their mistakes and they acted honorably." Instead of hiring lawyers and suing the hospital, the Ferreros settled for a sum of $800,000.

That became the seed money for the Sebastian Ferrero Foundation.

The Ferreros added much of their own money and began raising additional funds. They held a gala where they hoped to draw three hundred people. More than twice that many showed up. "The fire marshal had to put a cap on how many people could be there," says Horst. "So many people wanted to show their love and support." They organized charity runs and persuaded major corporations to match the funds they raised. They relied on social media to spread the word about the foundation, and they engaged supporters from across the state. Their initial goal was to raise five million dollars—and, remarkably, they got that much from just one bighearted donor. "We had so many events and we created so much awareness, and that's how it all moved forward," Horst says. "It was driven by passion."

Still, they knew that to realize their dream, they would need much more. The Ferreros arranged a meeting with the CEO of a health system in Gainesville, and the CEO praised their efforts and their persistence. But right after their first gala in 2008 he also threw cold water on their dream of a dedicated children's hospital.

"An economically sustainable children's hospital as part of the Shands system would be a wonderful asset," the CEO told the *Gainesville Sun*. But accomplishing that, he continued, "will take a number of years—if not a decade—and a much more favorable economic climate."

～～～

Seven years later, on Wednesday, September 3, 2014, a gentle breeze fluttered through the long, colorful ribbons hung outside a building on Archer Road. Hundreds of people were gathered there, including Horst and Luisa Ferrero and their children Sergio, Santiago, and Stefano.

They were all there to witness something special.

Speeches were given. Cheers rang through the crowd. The Ferreros and their children were handed an oversize pair of scissors and together cut a ceremonial ribbon.

The Sebastian Ferrero Atrium at the University of Florida Health Shands Children's Hospital was open.

The children's hospital, set within the larger University of Florida Health Shands campus, is one of the country's premier pediatric hospitals. When children arrive, they walk through the front doors and into the Sebastian Ferrero Atrium, a place of whimsy and wonder. There are interactive video displays, nature-themed art, an aquarium, and elevators that only children and their families can use. "It is not a frightening place," says Horst. "It is a place where children can feel calm and comfortable and happy."

In the middle of the atrium, there is a bright, beautiful sculpture on a white pedestal. It depicts a smiling boy in colorful green pants and an orange-striped shirt, reaching up to the sky to touch a butterfly shaped like a heart. It was created by world-renowned artist Romero Britto especially for the atrium, and it is called *Tomorrow*. It is a celebration, Britto explained, "of the well-being and happiness of children."

And on one wall of the atrium, there is a large framed photo.

It shows a boy, three years old, running and laughing and carefree, his smile as wide as the world.

"Sebastian," Horst says, "is the little hero who brought us all together."

~≈~

How did a project so large and daunting happen so quickly? How did the Ferreros overcome so many obstacles and entrenched industry practices? How could an event so unthinkably tragic turn into something so positive and beautiful?

The answer is a single word: Sebastian.

Horst and Luisa made the decision to honor their son's remarkable life by realizing the dream they had for him—that he would one day make a real difference in the world. And now, through their efforts, Sebastian has made a profound difference and will continue to make a difference for decades to come.

What the Ferreros created out of love for their son was magical. But what they managed to accomplish in such a short time did not happen by magic. It took hard work, determination, dedication, and twenty-hour days. Put simply, the Ferreros were relentless. They enlisted the help of all the people who had known and loved Sebastian—friends, neighbors, families, teachers, school administrators. They energized dedicated professionals to rally behind their cause—doctors, community leaders, university coaches, hospital officials, even Florida's two senators. Together they used their unique and considerable skills to raise millions of dollars. And they never stopped believing in the power of Sebastian's dream.

Instead of turning inward after the tragedy, they turned outward—and brought an entire community together around a common goal.

"That," says Luisa, "is the real legacy of Sebastian."

The Ferreros' mission—to create a culture of patient safety in hospitals everywhere—is ongoing. But their efforts have already produced remarkable results.

In 2008, the University of Florida's College of Medicine instituted a four-year quality and patient safety curriculum for all medical students—an initiative spurred by what happened to Sebastian and pushed by the Ferreros. The foundation hosts a series of family-friendly fund-raising events, including a car show, a town fair, and its annual *Noche de Gala* event, which continues to draw thousands of supporters every year. Horst and Luisa have also given many speeches to medical students and professionals, describing their ordeal and urging greater care and compassion.

"Listen to parents," is one of the concepts they stress. "Parents know their children better than anyone."

Then there is the hospital's top floor. It used to be the luxurious floor where the former hospital CEO and top administrators enjoyed lots of natural light and the best views of the University of Florida's campus. Today, it is a state-of-the-art pediatric cardiac intensive care unit that performs fifteen percent of all heart transplants in America and uses modern procedures for congenital heart diseases, even on artificial hearts.

"To see toddlers riding around on tricycles and exercising and recovering after a heart transplant while still hooked to their monitors is incredible," says Horst. "It feels miraculous, especially for those parents who now have hope in their eyes."

And all of it—all of it—is because of Sebastian.

"At every step, every milestone, I think about him," says Horst. "I think about how he is helping so many people. To see these children come through the hospital, and to see them happy and joyful, is all because of Sebastian."

Says Luisa, "When I get a phone call from parents, sharing their good experiences at the hospital and thanking us, I know this is the work of Sebastian. It is him—*he* is doing this. He has done more than I could ever do in my life, and he did it in just three years."

There is something else about Sebastian that is important to say. Sebastian is not gone. Sebastian is still here.

"He is everywhere," Luisa says. "He is such a big presence in my life. He is part of everything I do. Wherever I am, Sebastian is there, too."

He is there in the home movies his loving parents took of him—little Sebastian climbing on a stuffed elephant, chasing bubbles, splashing in the bathtub, twirling spaghetti around a big fork, tenderly kissing his baby brother Sergio.

He is there in the faces of the hundreds of children who pass through the atrium named for him, and in their smiles as they leave healthy and safe.

Sebastian is there in the home where his family lives, and where his younger brothers speak of him and ask to see his photos. Even Stefano, the youngest at six, will turn to his mother and say, "Tell me the name of the boy who was my brother."

And his mother will smile and say, "Sebastian."

Most of all, Sebastian is there in the hearts of those who love him, and who were inspired by him, and whose lives he changed forever.

"Sometimes I talk to him," Horst says. "There is a little memorial for him at his school, a collage of photos with his picture in the middle. And when I'd pass it, I would stop and talk to Sebastian. I would talk to him out loud."

"Sebastian," Horst would say to his boy, "we did it. We did it together."

There is an invisible thread that connects Sebastian Ferrero and his loved ones. But there are many more threads that connect him to the hundreds of children he helps every day—and even to all the children who will pass through his atrium, and see his cheerful face, in the years and decades to come.

Sebastian is, as his parents always knew, a child of the world.

RED BALLOONS

*One of the sweetest invisible thread stories I've ever come across starts
with a letter to Santa.*

*It was written by a five-year-old San Diego girl named Joie. As part
of a kindergarten project, Joie and her classmates wrote letters to Santa,
tied them to balloons, and released them into the sky.*

*"Dear Santa," Joie's letter read, "I would like to have a mermaid
doll with a bow for Christmas. Thank you. Love, Joie."*

*Joie's red balloon stayed up for hours before finally beginning its
descent. A man named Terry Hardin was leaving work when he looked
up and saw it coming toward him. For some reason he was mesmerized
by it, and he watched it for several minutes until it landed in a parking
lot a few feet away. He picked it up, read the note, and felt a chill.*

The note was written by a girl with the unusually spelled name Joie.

*Terry's mother, who had recently passed away, was also named
Joie.*

*Terry eventually tracked down the kindergartner and gave her a
Christmas gift—a Little Mermaid doll with a bow.*

But the real gift wasn't the doll.

*When Terry's mother passed away, his relationship with her was
strained. There were issues they hadn't resolved. Then a red balloon fell
out of the sky and wound up in his hands, as if his mother had steered
it straight to him.*

*As Terry told a San Diego news station, the red balloon "literally
came from heaven to make things right."*

*This story seems almost too good to be true. I mean, what are the
odds? Joie's balloon could have landed anywhere—on a highway, in a*

tree, on the fifty-yard line of a football field. Instead it hovered over Terry's head, long enough to get his attention, then slowly made its way to him. He had to be in the right place at the perfect time—and he was.

And then, in Terry's hands, the two Joies came together. They were generations apart—heck, worlds apart—but together they created something magical. Five-year-old Joie's innocent letter ended up healing a wound that Terry thought would never heal. Then Terry's kind gesture fulfilled a child's belief in the goodness of the world.

Some invisible force connected the two Joies and Terry to produce a moment of breathtaking beauty.

A few years ago, I'm not sure I would have seen that red balloon as the instrument of an otherworldly connection.

But the last five years have changed me, and so now I do. Getting to meet so many angels on earth and hear so many inspirational stories has made me more aware of the connectedness that binds us all together. I feel I have become more observant. More attentive. More open. More giving. More adventurous. More understanding of how I fit in the world.

More authentically myself.

Five years ago, when I named my book An Invisible Thread, I didn't really comprehend a key part of the proverb that inspired the title—that invisible threads may stretch and tangle, but they never break.

But Sebastian's story, and the story you're about to read, have opened my eyes to its true meaning. The love that connects us here on earth continues to connect us when we move on. It is boundless. It is unbreakable. It is never-ending.

Which is why the simplest acts of kindness fill our lives with the divine.

30

THE RAINBOW

So far, I've shared the stories of a group of remarkable people who reached out to tell me about the powerful connections in their lives. Now I'd like to share a story of my own.

When I was in my twenties, my mother, Marie, was stricken with uterine cancer. She bravely fought it and was determined to beat it. My father checked her into Memorial Sloan Kettering Hospital in Manhattan, which was only a few minutes from where I lived in New York City. I went to see her for a few hours after work every night. She was in and out of the hospital, until the day we found her unresponsive at home and rushed her to the emergency room.

When we arrived there, a priest stood by my mother and gave her last rites. My sister Annette and I watched her struggle to draw even a short breath. Then she stopped struggling. Her doctor, Dr. Ochoa, turned toward us. "She is gone," he said.

I felt a wave of emotions. I should have felt relief, because I knew my mother had been suffering terribly. But I felt a crushing sadness, because I knew my mother's life had been so hard. I was sad that her life hadn't been filled with more happiness.

My sister and I were still crying when something happened. Something that defied explanation.

Just a few minutes after she'd been pronounced dead, my mother started to breathe.

"Oh, my God, your mother is alive!" the nurse who noticed it first yelled out. "Talk to her, talk to her!"

And then my mother opened her eyes.

※

I was in shock. I didn't know what was happening. I looked at my mother, and she turned toward us and gave us a warm, peaceful, beautiful smile. The nurse took her vital signs, and they were stronger than they had been in months. At first my mother couldn't speak clearly, but suddenly she was lucid and alert, and she had something to say.

In a calm voice, she declared, "I have been given the strength to tell you everything I always wanted to say to you, but couldn't."

It was astonishing. I couldn't make sense of it. Neither could Dr. Ochoa, who offered no explanation. He had been absolutely certain when he'd pronounced her dead. But then she just . . . came back.

"I want to talk to all of you," my mother said.

We went to be with her one by one. My sister Annette went first, and then it was my turn. I tightly held my mother's hand.

"You have always been such a good daughter," she told me. "There were times when I didn't understand you, but I know you are strong and good."

This was true. I loved my mother to no end, but we also had our differences. I was headstrong and defiant, and we fought a lot. Through it all, however, we remained fiercely protective of, and devoted to, each other. Our bond was unbreakable.

"Laurie, I am so proud of you," my mother said to me from her hospital bed. "I love you very much."

Those were words every daughter hopes and prays and needs to hear.

My mother also spoke with my father and my brother Steven, and a bit later with my brother Frank and sister Nancy, who rushed to the hospital to be with her. When all our individual talks were done, my mother gathered us together and told us what had happened after Dr. Ochoa had pronounced her dead.

"I saw the other side," she explained. "It is far more beautiful and peaceful than we could ever imagine. I now know in my heart I will be able to take care of all of you from there. I will be able to look down and see how you are doing and make sure everything is well."

My mother was really clear and sharp, and seemingly in no pain at all, so we asked Dr. Ochoa if we could take her home. He told us we could. But when we mentioned it to her, she balked.

"I don't want to go home," she said simply. "I want to stay here until it is time to go to my new home."

Once again, we were all shocked. None of us had any time to process what was happening, but still, I wanted to believe my mother had just miraculously been healed. It didn't occur to me that her inexplicable recovery might only be temporary.

But that's what it was.

About two hours later, my mother spoke in Italian and said, "*Padre, vengo a casa pronto*"—Father, I am coming home. Then she asked that we all hold hands and say the Lord's Prayer together.

"Now everyone give me a big kiss and tell me you love me and leave me in peace," she said.

Then she closed her eyes and slipped into a coma.

Three days later, my mother passed away.

She was forty-seven years old.

In the months after my mother passed, I was too devastated to really think about what she had told us—that she would be able to watch over us from heaven.

It was a beautiful sentiment, to be sure, but I didn't think about it in practical terms. I didn't imagine my mother literally peering down through the clouds and watching our every move. In fact, I didn't really feel her presence. I thought about her all the time, and I prayed to her, but I no longer felt her in my life. She was gone now, and that was that.

Then, six months after she passed, I had a dream.

I had the dream the night before a really important job interview. While preparing dinner that night, I accidentally sliced my finger. I went to the hospital and needed eight stitches, but seeing all that blood—and being back in a hospital—unnerved me. I went to bed crying, and I finally fell asleep believing I couldn't possibly do well in the interview.

Then I had the dream. In the dream, I saw my mother standing near me, and I ran up to her. We kissed and hugged and I told her how much I loved and missed her. The sensation of my arms around her and of kissing her was uncannily real.

"Mom, did you hear?" I said. "I cut my finger."

My mother said, "Laurie, of course I know."

Then I told her I was worried about my big interview.

"Laurie, don't worry," she said. "You're going to do great in your interview, and you're going to get the job."

Then she kissed me again and said, "Now try and get a good night's sleep."

I woke up from the dream sobbing, then fell back asleep. The next morning, I felt strangely peaceful. I went in for my interview, bandaged finger and all, and when it was over I knew I'd done well. And just like my mother assured me in my dream, I got the job.

I know many people will say, "Oh, it was just a dream. It wasn't real." And I know there's no way I can prove it was anything *other* than a dream.

But I can say this: after the dream, my relationship with my mother—which I thought had ended when she died—not only continued but *deepened into something new and powerful.* You see, I understood that my mother had come to me in my dream because she knew I needed her. From that day forward, I have felt my mother's strong presence in my life. I have felt her watching over me, just as she promised. I have felt like she is *right here with me.*

And *no one* can tell me that isn't true.

The dream about my mother was a turning point in my life. From then on, I have simply accepted that my mother plays an important and continuing role in my life. Not just because of the values she instilled in me, but because I believe she is actively involved in guiding me down a certain path each and every day.

Over the last five years, my mother's presence has only seemed to get stronger.

But really, what's happened is that I've become more capable of sensing it. Not just feeling it, but seeing it in all the signs she sends me.

I remember one of my very first speaking events after *An Invisible Thread* was published. I was not a natural public speaker; as I've mentioned before, I was terrified of it. But there I was anyway, about to address a crowd of people at a Big Brothers Big Sisters of Family Services of Westchester event. I was beyond nervous but also grateful the crowd wasn't large.

Then, in the audience, I saw a little girl with curly, dark brown hair sitting across the way. There were people milling about, but for some reason my attention was drawn to this little girl. I noticed she was staring at me, too.

I walked over to where she was sitting and said, "Hi, my name is Laura. What's your name?"

"Maria," she said.

For a moment, I was speechless. My mother's name was Marie, but in Italian it was Maria, and lots of people called her that. Other people called her Mary. When the little girl told me her name, I instantly thought of my mother. I believe that was the reason I'd been drawn to the girl! It was my mother's way of letting me know she was with me that day. Sure enough, I suddenly felt peaceful and poised. I said goodbye to Maria and, a bit later, gave my speech. There were no nerves. There was only calm.

After that, I began talking to my mother before all my speeches. I'd start the night before, and talk some more in the car ride over. Always, I'd ask her to be there for me, to give me strength, to make the anxiety go away.

"And if you can," I'd say to my mother, "show me a sign that you're there."

And inevitably, someone at the event would come up to me and tell me her name was Marie or Maria or Mary. Not once or twice.

Every time.

Okay, some of you might say, isn't Mary a pretty common name? It used to be, but since the 1960s it's steadily become less popular. Today it's not even in the top one hundred most common baby names. Sure, there's always a chance that someone named Marie, Maria, or Mary will cross your path on any given day.

But there's also a really good chance that that *won't* happen.

And yet, to this day, it has never failed me.

There have been close calls. I gave a speech at a Jewish synagogue on Long Island, and driving to the event I was worried I wouldn't meet any Maries or Marias or Marys there, because it is such a Catholic name. Before my speech, the rabbi tested the microphone by singing "Strangers in the Night," my mother's least favorite song of all time. The association of that song and my mother was really strong for me, and I wondered if that was her way of letting me know she was there for me. But no, I told myself, that doesn't really count. It's not the same thing.

I shook a lot of hands before the speech, but no luck. Afterward, I signed copies of my book and met dozens of people, but still, no luck. When there were only three people left on line, I resigned myself to not hearing my mother's name that night.

But then, once again, I felt drawn to the third-to-last person in line. I didn't know why. Maybe it was because she was pretty, with beautiful dark hair like my mother. As she gave me her copy of the book to sign, I asked for her name so I could personalize it.

"I'm Marie," she said.

"Marie!" I said, with an enthusiasm she surely didn't understand. "What are you doing in a Jewish synagogue?"

"Oh," she said, "a friend happened to invite me at the last minute."

I hugged her and thanked her for being "my" Marie.

⁕

At another speaking engagement, on the car ride over, I asked my mother, "Hey, Mom, how about you show up early today? I'm really tired and I really want this one to go well, and it would be nice if I knew you were there from the beginning."

The *third* person I met at the event said, "Hi, I'm Marie."

I asked my mother to show up early for another event, but I wound up signing a stack of books before the speech instead of after, when I would have personally met the buyers. That left me thinking I'd have much less of a chance to meet a Marie, Maria, or

Mary. Then a waiter who was running around preparing for dinner yelled out to a server, "Hey, Marie, can you help with these plates?"

Even when I made a TV appearance, the makeup artist was named Marie.

I have given well over one hundred fifty speeches and taped many TV appearances, and it has never failed. And every time it happens, I know in my heart—without the tiniest shred of doubt—that my mother is right there with me, right by my side.

Hearing her name is not the only way I know my mother is around. A very dear friend of mine, Laura Lynne Jackson—who has helped me so much on my spiritual journey, and whom I can never repay—once told me that my mother shows me rainbows as a way to signal that she is there. Not just traditional rainbows in the sky, but all kinds of different rainbows in different places. It is always up to me, however, to see them.

One day, I was at a really important meeting in a conference room, and I knew there were no Maries there. I said to myself, "Please, Mom, let me know you are here. Show me something spectacular. Show me something out of the ordinary, so I'll know you're here."

At that instant, I turned my head and looked out the conference room window at a parking lot. And there, I saw a giant rainbow. Not in the sky.

In the parking lot.

Now *that* is something out of the ordinary.

It was actually an enormous rainbow painted on a huge sign. Still, it was spectacular. And since I was sitting at the head of the table, I was the only one of several participants who could look out the window and see it.

Ever since then, I have seen a lot of rainbows in all sorts of places, and they have become another way my mother lets me know she's around.

There is a story in *An Invisible Thread* about a brown paper bag. Early in my friendship with Maurice, I usually met him only on Monday nights. As time went on, I would see him on some Saturdays, too. One Saturday, the buzzer in my apartment sounded. The doorman told me Maurice was in the lobby. I had him send Maurice up, and when he saw me he said, "I'm sorry to bother you, but I'm really hungry. Can we get something to eat?" I realized our Monday nights together weren't enough. So over lunch Maurice and I came up with a plan.

I told Maurice I could either give him money to buy food throughout the week, or I could prepare lunch for him and leave it with my doorman for Maurice to pick up. The choice was entirely his.

Maurice thought about it for a while.

"If you make me lunch," he asked, "will you put it in a brown paper bag?"

I wasn't sure what he was asking.

"Do you want it in a brown paper bag?" I said.

Maurice nodded.

"Miss Laurie, I don't want your money," he said. "I just want lunch in a brown paper bag."

"Okay, sure," I said. "But why?"

"Because when I see kids come to school with their lunch in a paper bag," Maurice said, "that means someone cares about them."

To me, a paper bag was just a paper bag. But to Maurice, it was a symbol. It had *meaning*. It was a physical representation of things that can't be seen—kindness, compassion, love.

In this way, Maurice taught me a profound lesson. He taught me that even the simplest, most ordinary objects and gestures and events can have an enormous impact on our lives, if we truly open our eyes and our hearts to what lies behind them.

Not too long ago, I gave a speech at an event that went quite well. I even received a standing ovation. Afterward, I was with my publicist and great friend Linda Michalisin, passing through a walkway at the hotel where I was staying, on the way to get my luggage.

I turned to Linda and said, "I bet my mother is proud of me."

No sooner had the words come out than I noticed something on the floor of the walkway. The entire hotel was pristine, and the walkway was spotless, except for this one thing. As I got closer, it looked like an ordinary piece of trash. But it wasn't. Not at all.

It was a brown paper bag.

I had told the story of the brown paper bag that day, and when I saw the bag on the ground I thought about Maurice. Then I picked it up to examine it. It was flat and unused. I turned it over, and what I saw left me breathless.

There was a colored drawing on the bag.

The drawing was of a big, beautiful rainbow.

"Well, how about that?" I thought. "I guess my mother really is proud of me."

I still have that little paper bag, and I will cherish it always.

EPILOGUE

When I celebrated my fiftieth birthday, I was surrounded by friends and family. I danced to some of my favorite songs and listened with tears in my eyes as some of my loved ones offered me toasts. The final toast, however, was special. It came from Maurice.

The boy who didn't think he'd live to see eighteen was now a man with a wife and a family. He wore a sharp black tuxedo, and his wife was in a beautiful blue gown. He came to the front of the room and took the microphone in his hand. He looked at me and smiled, and I smiled back.

"The way we met was so special to me," Maurice began. "I was a young boy on the street with barely nothing, and I was very hungry that day, and I asked this lady, 'Miss, can you spare some change?' And she walked away. And then she stopped . . . and she came back and took me to McDonald's.

"You know, at that moment, she saved my life. 'Cause I was going down the wrong road, the wrong hill . . . and the Lord sent me an angel.

"And my angel was Laurie."

I have always treasured that moment, and I even wrote about it in my first book. But it wasn't until recently that I thought back on it and realized Maurice had referred to me as his angel.

Back then, I thought he meant it in the way most people mean it when they call someone an angel—as in, "Oh, you're such an angel." But that's not what Maurice meant. He knew, long before I did, that there are angels on earth. It took me more than a decade to catch up—in fact, it took hearing all the stories in this book—but today I'm right there with him.

And when I get the chance to toast Maurice sometime soon, I'll be sure to steal a line from his speech and change it just a little: "The Lord sent me an angel, and my angel was Maurice."

Most of the stories in this book feature tiny moments, common events, and ordinary things. A self-help book. A garage door opener. A lost wallet. An unwanted rabbit. A hug. Yet all of these things, coupled with an act of kindness, wound up changing someone's life, and sometimes *many* lives.

The stories I've shared with you in this book have taught me that when we perform an act of kindness, we tap into an awesome power. Kindness *activates* the invisible thread connections among us. Kindness *gets things moving*.

Kindness makes us angels.

I believe these threads draw us to certain people and steer us on a certain path, but that is only the beginning of our journeys. It is then up to us to make something happen. It is up to us to take action.

And when that action is kindness—when it's grounded in love and compassion and empathy—we can change the world. One person at a time.

Every story in this book has taught me something new. But together, they have convinced me that we all have the power and promise to be angels. The story of Sebastian Ferrero taught me that the invisible threads that bind us do not end when we pass from this life. My mother's story taught me that we never stop being angels—we just become stealthier.

The powerful connections between us are real. They bring meaning to our lives. And the action that ignites them is kindness. We don't have to overhaul our lives or make radical changes to experience the great blessings they bring. All we have to do is think differently.

All we have to do is *believe*.

Believe that we are all connected by invisible threads.

Believe that a red balloon—or a garage door opener or a brown paper bag or a rainbow—doesn't have to be only what it is.

Believe that our lives can be bigger, better, bolder, more loving, more authentic, and more filled with genuine joy once we accept that we are the angels the world so desperately needs.

Acknowledgments

I n November 2011, I was so blessed to have my first book, *An Invisible Thread*, published and at the time I never imagined I was about to embark on the most fulfilling journey. The outpouring of love and support from my family, friends, and readers is truly remarkable and I will be forever grateful.

Thank you, Maurice Mazyck, for changing my life in so many extraordinary ways. I would love to also thank your wife, Michelle, and your beautiful children, Ikeem, Maurice, Jr., Jalique, Princess, Jahleel, Precious, and Jahmed.

Angels on Earth all began when I asked readers to share their own invisible thread stories with me. Still I never expected such an overwhelming response from readers all across the country and around the world. I only wish I could have included all of them in this book. To those whose stories were included, thank you for allowing and entrusting me to share your loving and inspiring invisible thread moments in this book. It is my hope that readers will continue to share acts of kindness and that these threads of kindness will continue to stretch around the world.

My deepest thanks to "my" angels on earth: Vicki Sokolik, Dru Sanchez, Laura Lahey Chambers, Talia Bardash, Dr. Jody Bardash, Michele Bardash, Chuck Posternak, Annie McCormick Bonner, Linda DeCarlo, LaJuana Moser, Jim Kettlewell, Avital

ACKNOWLEDGMENTS

Sutin, Rachel Sutin, Jason Bradburn, Jose Luis Balleza, Wendell
Affield, Angie Hawk, Eileen Pacheco Schwartz, Dr. Hipolito,
Dr. Dale Atkins, Susan Sagan Levitan, Barbara Campbell, Lou
Honderich, Christine Honderich, Linda Preuss, Jessica Preuss,
Tom Grotticelli, Iris Astrof, Debbie Ring, Nancy Kropacek, Mary
Schell, Eliza Marie Schell, Rose Mary Knudson, Barbara Ginsberg,
Debbie Shore, Billy Shore, Anne Houseman, Clay Dunn, Robin
Tartarkin, Mary Faulkner, Santino Faulkner, Deb Howe Allen,
Solomon Young, Andy Smallman, Genevieve Piturro, Monique
Cano, Mary Warwick, Mary Phillips, Lucy Galasso, Dr. Angel B.
Pérez, and Horst and Luisa Ferrero.

My deepest thanks will always be to my beloved mother, Marie
Procino Carino, who has been by my side showing me her everlasting love and presence through rainbows. Thank you for letting
me know you are with me by always having a Marie, Maria, or
Mary in the audience at my speaking engagements, television
appearances, and in my daily life. You have never failed to show
up! There are also six stories in *Angels on Earth* with my mother's
name. My mother knows I feel her presence and she loves letting
me know at the most appropriate moments that she is with me.
Thank you, Mom, for giving me the strength, courage, and the
confidence I have needed to go on this remarkable journey.

To my father, who knows I love and forgive him. Thank you for
being so generous to share your strengths with me. A very special
thanks to my beloved brother Frank for coming on my journey with
me and for showing me in simple ways how you are by my side. It
brings me enormous comfort to know you are at peace in Heaven.

I am beyond blessed to have the most wonderful family who
gives me endless love and support and encouragement—my sisters Annette Carino Lubsen and Nancy Carino Johansen, and my
loving brother Steven Carino, who are my biggest fans.

Thank you to their amazing families: Annette's husband, Bruce Lubsen, their daughter Colette Lubsen Reid and her husband, Mike, and their daughters Calli and Sadie; Derek Lubsen, his wife, Brooke, and their children, Dashiell, Heidi, and Violet; Brooke Lubsen Cassens, her husband, Steve, and their children Chase and Evelyn; Nancy's husband, John Johansen, and their beautiful children Jena and Christian; and to my sweet poodles, Coco and Emma, for keeping me grounded and company every day. I hope you know I treasure and love all of you very much.

My everlasting gratitude for the support of my mother's brothers, Pat and John Procino, and her sister, Diana Robedee and their families.

Six years ago, I met with my cowriter Alex Tresniowski at the Stardust Diner in New York City and shared the story of my friendship with Maurice. Alex and I both worked at Time Inc. for seventeen years, yet our paths never crossed. We traveled in the same elevator bank every day and ate in the same cafeteria, and still we never met. But luckily *An Invisible Thread* brought us together. Alex is the most beautiful writer and there are no words to express how deeply I respect his remarkable talent and care about our friendship. I never could have imagined at our first meeting how he would become such an integral part of my life. Alex is one of the dearest friends anyone could ever dream to have: thoughtful, kind, and beyond generous. I believe my mother and his mother once again orchestrated our friendship from Heaven. They both knew we needed each other!

Thanking Nena Madonia-Oshman at Dupree/Miller does not seem fitting enough, as it does not truly describe my deepest appreciation to her for being the most incredibly supportive, passionate, and encouraging agent and great friend. Nena's relentless drive and determination to make a difference in the

ACKNOWLEDGMENTS

lives of others' is a beautiful gift. I will also be forever grateful to Jan Miller and her amazing team at Dupree/Miller for supporting *An Invisible Thread*, *An Invisible Thread Christmas Story*, and *Angels on Earth*. All of this would not have been possible if Jan had not first believed in our story back in 2010.

For the past six years I have had the honor and great pleasure to work with Jonathan Merkh at Howard Books. Jonathan, you are an amazing publisher and, along with Judith Curr, president and publisher of Atria Books, and Carolyn Reidy, president & CEO at Simon & Schuster, you have embraced my books and have given me the most talented and dedicated teams to work with. So thank you both from the bottom of my heart!

A very special thanks to my editor, Beth Adams, at Howard Books. You believed in *Angels on Earth* from its inception and you have been such a supportive champion. Thank you for your thoughtful and brilliant edit suggestions. You are truly remarkable and I am so fortunate to work along side you. A very special thanks to the entire team at Howard Books and at Simon & Schuster, including Rob Birkhead, Jessica Chin, Bruce Gore, Lisa Keim, Michelle Leo, Brandi Lewis, Ami McConnell, Katie Sandell, and Jennifer Smith. Thank you, Valerie Garfield, and everyone at Simon & Schuster for your incredible dedication and support of *An Invisible Thread Christmas Story*.

The title of my first book comes from an ancient Chinese proverb: an invisible thread connects those who we are destined to meet. I am so enormously blessed to have so many invisible thread connections that continue to enrich my life.

Thank you, Sheri Wohl-Lapidus, for your friendship and for recommending and introducing me to one of my dearest friends and most important people in my life—Linda Michalisin, my publicist and marketing strategist. Linda, thank you for relentlessly working with such extraordinary passion, insight, and love. You are my "partner in crime" and there are no words to describe my deepest appreciation for your brilliant work and for always encouraging and pushing me to do better. You continue to enhance my life every day. My deepest thanks to Linda's husband, Bill, and their children, Liam and Ella for sharing their mornings, days, and late nights with me.

Over the past five years I have been so fortunate to work with the amazing teams at Simon & Schuster Speakers Bureau and Greater Talent Network. This part of my journey is one I never anticipated and I cannot begin to express my deepest appreciation for their unrelenting support. I will be forever grateful to Hadley Walker for her unyielding dedication and steadfast support. Hadley, thank you for believing in me from the beginning. Thank you also to Jennifer Peykar, Edna Schenkel, and Jillian Conroy, and to the teams who continue to support and cheer me on.

In 2008, Laura Lynne Jackson came into—and changed—my life. Laura's gifts to the universe are amazing and I have seen first-hand how she enriches the lives of others. Laura has helped me believe how our loved ones never truly leave us and continually show us signs—as long as we are willing to open up our minds and hearts to see them. Laura, your beauty and light have shown me how my mom, "my Marie, Maria, and Mary," is always with me. So thank you my treasured friend.

I am so blessed to have so many wonderful friends who have been with me through my ups and downs and are like family to me. I am enormously blessed by their overwhelming goodness and I can only hope I have come close to returning their love and friendship. A heartfelt thanks to Christina Albee and Gregg Goldsholl and their sweet daughters, Clare and Grace; Debbie and Russell Brown; Paul and Pam Caine; Donna and Lou Cona;

ACKNOWLEDGMENTS

Lori, Michael, Syndey, and Darien Cohn; Silvana Constantinides
and Lila and Juliette Smith; Yvette Manessis Corporon, Hope
Falkenberg-Coughlin, June Deane, Mary Gallagher-Vassilakos,
David Geithner, Susan Goldfarb, Barbara Groner-Robinton,
Cherie and Joseph Guccione, Lori Ressa-Kyle, Peggy Mansfield,
Nora and Ed McAniff, Martha Nelson, Darcy Parriott-Phillips,
Brette Popper and Paul Spraos, Lauren Price, Andrea Rogan,
Phoebe Rothkopf, Valerie Salembier, Kim Schechter, Cindy
Schreibman, Janet Shechter, Sara Shubert, Lori Levine-Silver,
Sue and John Spahlinger, Stacie Sullivan, Lynn Ruane-Tuttle,
Sandi Shurgin-Werfel, Kevin White, and Raul Barreneche.

Every young girl dreams of how one day she will be presented
with the iconic blue box with a white satin bow. I was definitely
that girl. Over the past six years I have had the privilege to
work at Tiffany & Co., and I would like to thank my friends for
their incredible support and for accommodating my demanding
schedule.

My website has allowed me to connect in a very special way
with my readers and for that I would like to thank Kristina and
J Wadsworth.

A very special thanks to my brilliant and talented photogra-
pher, Jennifer Tonetti Spellman, my hair stylist for over eighteen
years, Liell Hilligoss at Pierre Michel, and Kristen Colasrdo at
BÙ-TIQUE.

I would also like to thank the many people who have invited
me to speak at their events and schools, and all the audiences
who have listened to my story. I will be forever grateful for your
amazing love and support of *An Invisible Thread* and *An Invisible
Thread Christmas Story*.

Finally, thank you to everyone who has read my books and
shared my journey—you are my true advocates and the reason

why I keep telling my story. Over the past six years, I have learned there is so much goodness in our world, so many people who show kindness each and every day without expecting anything in return. My hope is the true stories in *Angels on Earth* will inspire readers across the country and around the world to share the same vision and become angels themselves.

—*Laura Schroff*

First, foremost, and once again, thank you to Laura Schroff, for taking me along on her beautiful journey. Laura, I've learned so much from you, about grace and goodness and loyalty. But the biggest blessing of all has been your friendship. It's been an amazing, amazing trip. Thank you also to my buddy and fellow Knicks fan Maurice Mazyck, who has such a good heart, and to publicist and marketing strategist Linda Michalisin, for her round-the-clock hustle. Thank you to Nena Madonia Oshman and Jan Miller, my great literary agents, for making this book happen, and to Jonathan Merkh, Beth Adams, Bruce Gore, Jennifer Smith, Lisa Keim, and the rest of the team at Howard Books, for their powerful belief in invisible threads. A big thank-you to Carolyn Reidy and Valerie Garfield for making Simon & Schuster such a wonderful home. And I can't forget Will Becker, who's been a real pal, and Mark Apovian, my oldest and funniest friend.

I wouldn't be anywhere without my family, an incredible collection of people I love—my big sis Tamara and her dancing guy, Howie; my wise and welcoming sister Fran and her husband, Rich, and their (awesome and all grown-up) kids Emily and Zach; my cooler-than-me brother Nick and his wife, Susan, and their soccer-loving son, Humboldt; and also Earlene and Grace and

ACKNOWLEDGMENTS

Willie and Jessie and Paul and Markie and Janice and Sammy and Dino and Holly and Andreas and Cindy and Jordan and Chelsea and especially my beautiful niece Celeste (I want fun gum!) and my dino-digging nephew Charlie (I try?). And of course, the little gang that lives in my heart and eats my bananas: Manley, Guy, Lady, BiBi, JoJo, Nino, She She, Baby Girl, and Bitsy. You guys give me so much love. Finally, to Lorraine Kay Stundis. Rainey, you're the star that always guides me in the right direction.

—*Alex Tresniowski*

These wonderful organizations, mentioned in this book, help everyday people become angels on earth. For more information, please visit the following websites.

Vicki Sokolik
Starting Right, Now
www.startingrightnow.org

Chuck Posternak
Big Brothers Big Sisters of America
www.bigsnyc.org

Andy Smallman
www.andysmallman.com

Deb Allen
The Fresh Air Fund
www.freshair.org

Debbie Shore
Share Our Strength
www.nokidhungry.org

Eileen Pacheco Schwartz
ChildFund International
www.childfund.org

WEBSITES IN BOOK

Jason Bradburn
Be The Match
www.bethematch.org

Genevieve Piturro
Pajama Program
www.pajamaprogram.org

Horst and Luisa Ferrero
Sebastian Ferrero Foundation
www.sebastianferrero.org

Laura would love to connect with you.

www.lauraschroff.com
Facebook/LauraSchroff
@aninvisibletrd

Read where Laura's inspiring story started in her
#1 New York Times and international bestseller

An INVISIBLE
THREAD

An Invisible Thread is a compelling book with a life-changing message. It is a true modern day story that serves as a model for how we can all make a difference by sharing small acts of kindness.

"If you have a beating heart—or if you fear you're suffering a hardening of the emotional arteries—you really ought to commit to this book at the earliest possible opportunity …read this book. And pass it on. And encourage the next reader to do the same." —JESSE KORNBLUTH, *HUFFINGTON POST*

An Invisible Thread Christmas Story is a heartwarming children's book capturing the true meaning of the holidays. It is a sweet reminder that a gift from the heart is always the best present of all.

**Available wherever books are sold
or at SimonandSchuster.com**

 HOWARD BOOKS®
AN IMPRINT OF SIMON & SCHUSTER, INC.
A CBS COMPANY